A Practical Guide to Short Marriages for Family Lawyers

Second Edition

Sadie Glover is a Family Law Partner and Mediator based in South Buckinghamshire. Her practice encompasses all aspects of family law, with a particular emphasis on complex financial remedy and children matters. She recently acted in the published decisions of *M v F* [2024] EWFC 393 and *M v F* [2024] EWFC 393 (No 2) (costs), instructing Beth.

Sadie regularly delivers training for MBL Ltd, one of the country's leading CPD providers. She is also a committed and active member of Resolution, sitting as Secretary to the Buckinghamshire and Berkshire Regional Committee.

Philip Perrins is a specialist matrimonial finance barrister at 1GC | Family Law with expertise in international cases, including disputed divorce jurisdiction, forum disputes, Part III applications, and marital status cases. He recently acted in *Boughajdim v Hayoukane (Validity of Foreign Marriage)* [2022] EWHC 2673 (Fam), *J v A* [2023] EWFC 132 (jurisdiction and forum dispute), *Mahtani v Mahtani (Validity of Foreign Divorce)* [2023] EWHC 2988 (Fam) and, with Beth, in *Mahtani v Mahtani (No. 2) (Adverse Inferences)* [2025] EWFC 35 (Fam). He is often instructed in cases involving third party claims, having appeared in the leading case of *Fisher Meredith v JH and PH* [2012] 2 FLR 536.

Philip is also qualified arbitrator and conducts arbitrations under the IFLA Scheme, as well as sitting as pFDR evaluator.

Beth Hibbert is a specialist family barrister at 1GC | Family Law, instructed on cases across the full spectrum of family law, with a growing reputation in financial remedies work. She was recently instructed by Sadie in the published cases of *M v F* [2024] EWFC 393 and *M v F* [2024] EWFC 393 (No 2) (costs) and appeared with Philip in *Mahtani v Mahtani (No. 2) (Adverse Inferences) [2025] EWFC 35 (Fam)*, in which court made a lump sum order in favour of the wife of £13.9m having drawn adverse inferences as to the likely extent of the husband's wealth due to his non-engagement and non-disclosure.

A Practical Guide to Short Marriages for Family Lawyers

Second Edition

Sadie Glover LLB (Hons), Solicitor

Philip Perrins LLB (Hons), LLM (Cantab), of the Middle Temple, Barrister

Beth Hibbert BA (Oxon), MSc, of Lincoln's Inn, Barrister

Law Brief Publishing

Published 2025 by Law Brief Publishing, an imprint of Law Brief Publishing Ltd
30 The Parks
Minehead
Somerset
TA24 8BT

www.lawbriefpublishing.com

Paperback: 978-1-916698-78-9

FOREWORD

This invaluable practical guide is essential reading for all of those who practice financial remedies law.

A Practical Guide to Short Marriages (Second edition) will be a go-to book for short marriage cases. The authors outline comprehensive guidance on calculating the duration of a marriage, the application of the needs, sharing and compensation principles in short marriage cases, and how the issues of housing, maintenance, pensions and agreements may be considered following a short marriage.

Since the publication of the first edition of this book, several seminal cases have grappled with the financial remedies exercise following short marriages, including *VV v VV* [2022] EWFC 41, *Butler v Butler* [2023] EWFC 2453 and *Helliwell v Entwistle* [2024] EWHC 740 (Fam). Another update in the field of financial remedies law is the publication of the Report of the Pension Advisory Group: A Guide to the Treatment of Pensions on Divorce (second edition) (January 2024). This book provides succinct analysis of the updating authorities as well as a deeper look at the more historical cases.

I have little doubt you enjoy reading the book and find it indispensable.

Janet Bazley KC
1GC | Family Law
March 2025

PREFACE

We would like to thank Garry and his team at Law Brief Publishing Ltd for making this project happen and Janet Bazley KC for her kind words in the foreword to this 2nd Edition.

The law stated here is accurate, to the best of our knowledge and belief, as at 20 March 2025.

Sadie Glover
Philip Perrins,
Beth Hibbert
March 2025

CONTENTS

CHAPTER ONE

INTRODUCTION: WHAT IS A SHORT MARRIAGE AND WHY IS IT RELEVANT?

The Matrimonial Causes Act 1973 lists the matters to which the Court is to have regard in determining how to exercise its powers to make financial orders on divorce. One of these factors is "the duration of the marriage"[1]. This chapter will consider why the duration of the marriage is relevant to the approach of the Family Court when determining a financial remedies application.

According to the ONS data released on 22 February 2024[2] in 2022 the median duration of marriage at divorce was 12.9 years for opposite-sex divorces. For those with less than 30 years of marriage, the most common duration of marriage for opposite-sex couples getting divorced in 2022 was 7 years, with 4,143 divorces.

For same-sex divorces in 2022, the median duration of marriage was 7.5 years for male same-sex couples and 6.3 years for female same-sex couples, although same-sex divorces have only been possible in England and Wales since 2015. The most common duration of marriage for male same-sex couples in 2022 was 10 to 14 years (81 divorces), and 6 years for female same-sex couples (121 divorces).

The length of the marriage will have a potentially significant impact on the claims of the parties arising from divorce. A claim arising after a long

1 Matrimonial Causes Act 1973, s 25(2)(d).

2 https://www.ons.gov.uk/peoplepopulationandcommunity/birthsdeathsandmarriages/divorce/bulletins/divorcesinenglandandwales/2022

marriage is likely to be far greater than one arising after a marriage of one or two years. This is principally because in shorter marriages, there will have been less time than in longer marriages for the parties to accrue matrimonial wealth, become accustomed to the standard of living of the marriage and generate needs, although the presence of children in a short marriage can have a monumental impact in relation to needs.

Central to every financial remedy case is s25 (2) of the Matrimonial Causes Act 1973, the 's25 factors'. Equivalent provision is set out in Schedule 5 Part 5 to the Civil Partnership Act 2004 at paragraph 21 (2).

The power of the court to make financial orders arising from a divorce is derived from the provisions of Part II of the Matrimonial Causes Act 1973. The court has the power to make any or all of the following orders:

- Periodical payments
- Secured periodical payments
- Lump sum
- Property adjustment
- Variation of settlement
- Pension sharing

In exercising its powers, the court must have regard to "all the circumstances of the case", as well as to a list of specifically identified matters. The first consideration must be given to the welfare of any children, and thereafter to the matters set out in s25(2)(a) – (h) MCA 1973.

The s 25 factors are not formulaic and not listed in any order of importance. They are simply a list of relevant considerations the court must refer to when deciding a case. They can be summarised as comprising:

a) The resources available to both parties, extant and/or reasonably foreseeable;

b) The financial needs of the parties;

c) The standard of living enjoyed by the parties;

d) The parties ages and the length of the marriage, and any disabilities;

e) The contributions of each party;

f) The conduct of each party;

g) Any benefit either part will lose as a result of the divorce.

In reality, the application of the s25 factors could lead different judges on different days to various different conclusions, even if the facts are the same, all of which could fall well within the scope of their vast judicial discretion.

In ***Miller v Miller; McFarlane v McFarlane***[3] the House of Lords identified and developed three key principles and extra-statutory factors in respect of financial remedy proceedings to be considered in all cases alongside the s 25 factors, namely: needs, sharing and compensation. The principles of needs, sharing and compensation apply equally in short marriages as in longer marriages, but the duration of the marriage will impact on the court's application of the principles. Please see Chapter Two for more details.

3 [2006] UKHL 24, [2006] 2 AC 618, paragraph 11.

The duration of the marriage is relevant to the court's task of distributing the parties' assets because it is directly relevant to the level of parties' financial dependence on one another, and to the period that the parties have had to accumulate matrimonial assets.

After a long marriage of say 20-years, during which the parties' finances have been mixed and mingled and one spouse may have become dependent on the other, it would be grossly unfair not to distribute the assets in order to meet both parties' needs, and share any excess.

However, after a very short marriage, it may well be fair for the court to treat the parties as if, in effect, they had never been married at all and order no financial award, particularly if there are no children of the marriage and the parties are young.

For example, in the case of ***Krystman v Krystman***[4], a case in which the marriage lasted just two weeks, with the wife applying for a financial remedy 25 years after separation, the Court of Appeal considered that no order was appropriate. The parties had similar incomes, with the husband supporting himself and his new wife with £1,300 per annum, and the wife supporting herself with £1,500 per annum. At first instance, the judge ordered the husband to pay the wife £75 per annum on a joint lives' basis. The husband's appeal was allowed, and the wife's application was dismissed. In all of the circumstances, given that there was a mere fortnight of cohabitation, no children, a 26-year separation and no attempt by either party to make any contact, the court found that the husband should not be required to make any financial provision for the wife. Even a nominal order would not be appropriate because if the husband came into wealth unexpectedly, it would not be fair for the wife to have any share in it.

The court is duty bound per section 25A(1) of the Matrimonial Causes Act 1973 to consider whether a clean break order should be made in all

4 [1973] 1 WLR 927.

cases, regardless of the duration of the marriage. However, a clean break is often more likely to be deemed appropriate or desirable in a short marriage case, in which there will have been less time for the marriage to generate needs which must be met on an ongoing basis.

Ultimately, the issues surrounding short marriages and how the duration of the marriage affects the division of assets can bring a number of difficulties, particularly with regard to when a marriage started and ended, meeting needs after a short marriage, and the sharing of matrimonial and non-matrimonial assets after the breakdown of a short marriage. This book will seek to examine these issues relating to short marriages in an accessible manner to assist practitioners dealing with short marriage cases.

CHAPTER TWO

HOW TO ASSESS THE LENGTH OF A MARRIAGE

2.1 How short is a 'short marriage'?

There is no statutory definition of a short marriage, and as such, it is necessary to refer to the relevant case law. It is generally accepted that a marriage of less than 5 years will be regarded by the court as short.

There are some borderline cases which describe 6-7 year marriages as short, including:

- In ***Sharp v Sharp***[5], the parties cohabited from the end of 2007, married in June 2009 and separated in December 2013. Singer J, the judge at first instance, described the marriage of 6 years as "*not so desperately short … as some, but still by no means lengthy*". The Court of Appeal reaffirmed that the marriage was indeed a short one.

- In ***H v H***[6], the parties cohabited from June 1997 and regarded themselves as married from September 1998 after a Spanish marriage ceremony. They were legally married in September 2003 and separated in the first half of 2005. The marriage of almost 8 years was described by Singer J as "*a relatively short marriage comprising cohabitation over around 7 years*"[7].

---

5 [2017] EWCA Civ 408, [2017] 2 FLR 1095.

6 [2009] EWHC 494 (Fam), [2009] 2 FLR 795.

7 See paragraph 13.

- In ***R v R***[8] the parties cohabited from March 2002, married in August 2002 and separated in January 2009. Coleridge J described the 7-year marriage as a "*short-ish marriage case*"[9].

- In ***FF v KF***[10], the parties commenced their relationship in 2004, became engaged and planned their marriage ceremony for 27 December 2007, but separated three days before the ceremony. The parties reconciled in October 2010, cohabited from April 2011, married in October 2011 and separated in September 2013. Despite the 9-year off and on relationship, Mostyn J noted, "*everyone seems to have been content to have characterised this as a "short marriage"...*"[11].

There is therefore some scope for discretion as to what counts as a short marriage, and, as ever, the court's assessment of the duration of the marriage will depend on the circumstances of the case.

In any event, the duration of the marriage is just one of the factors that the court considers relevant alongside the other factors at s 25(2) of the Matrimonial Causes Act 1973.

2.2 When does a marriage start?

2.2.1 Establishing cohabitation as marriage

Historically, the court considered the duration of the marriage to be the length of time between the date of the marriage to the date of the breakdown. Only in exceptional circumstances would the court take into account periods of pre-marital cohabitation. However, over the last four

8 [2013] EWHC 3093, [2013] 1 FLR 120.

9 See paragraph 9.

10 [2017] EWHC 1093 (Fam).

11 See paragraph 5.

decades, case law has firmly established that any premarital cohabitation will be added to the length of the marriage, when the court assesses the duration of the marriage. Now pre-marital cohabitation may be treated as either extending the duration of the marriage, or as a circumstance of the case to be taken into account more generally.

One of the most significant cases involving premarital cohabitation is ***GW v RW***[12], in which the parties had married in April 1989 after cohabiting for around 18 months. In 1995 the parties separated for 18 months before reconciling and cohabiting for a further a 5 years. The wife petitioned for divorce in 2001. Mr N Mostyn QC (as he then was, sitting as a Deputy High Court Judge) concluded that it would be unfair not to include the period of cohabitation preceding the marriage in the duration of the marriage where there had been no major change in the way in which the parties lived during and after the marriage. Further, it would not be right to include in the duration of the marriage the period in which there had been a formal and defined separation. Therefore, the duration of the marriage was determined to be just over 12 years. Mr Mostyn said at paragraph 33:

> "*... The case of White v White has emphasised that the law in this area is not moribund but must move to reflect changing social values. I cannot imagine anyone nowadays seriously stigmatising pre-marital cohabitation as 'living in sin' or lacking the quality of emotional commitment assumed in marriage. Thus, in my judgment,* ***where a relationship moves seamlessly from cohabitation to marriage without any major alteration in the way the couple live, it is unreal and artificial to treat the periods differently.*** *On the other hand, if it is found that the pre-marital cohabitation was on the basis of a trial period to see if there was any basis for later marriage then I would be of the view that it would not be right to include it as part of the 'duration of the marriage'.*" (emphasis added).

12 [2003] EWHC 611 (Fam), [2003] 2 FLR 108.

In ***Co v Co***[13] the parties cohabited for 8 years before a 4-year marriage. Coleridge J determined that the 8 year period of cohabitation should be given full weight where it "*seamlessly and immediately pre-dated the marriage*". He noted that pre-marital cohabitation cannot be ignored in assessing "*all of the other circumstances of the case*" per s25(1) MCA 1973, and in seeking to achieve fairness between the parties. Therefore, assets accrued during premarital cohabitation would in some cases be treated as matrimonial.

Following ***GW v RW***[14] and ***Co v Co***[15], it is standard for any period of premarital cohabitation to be added to the length of a marriage. The commencement of cohabitation in a settled relationship may well be treated as the appropriate start date of the marriage. This approach reflects changes in social mores and the fact that many people now choose to live together prior to marriage or civil partnership.

In ***C v C***[16] Moylan J acknowledged that in practice it can be difficult to establish a clearly defined start date of a committed pre-marital relationship and the court will not waste time investigating the precise date of cohabitation. He noted at paragraph 62:

> "*Parties should not be encouraged to expect the courts to enter into any extensive investigation of the nature of their premarital relationship many years later. It can also raise issues which do not appear in the Matrimonial Causes Act 1973 in specific terms and over which there could be an active debate in the search of the precise definitions.*"

---

13 [2004] EWHC 287, [2004] 1 FLR 1095.

14 [2003] EWHC 611 (Fam), [2003] 2 FLR 108.

15 [2004] EWHC 287, [2004] 1 FLR 1095.

16 [2007] EWHC 2033 (Fam), [2009] 1 FLR 8.

2.2.2 Examples: where pre-martial relationship is not included in the duration of the marriage

In ***McCartney v Mills-McCartney***[17] Bennett J found that before their marriage, the parties had a close relationship, spent many nights together, holidayed together and became engaged, but that the relationship was not "*a settled committed relationship moving seamlessly into marriage*" in circumstances where the wife had purchased a property for herself with the benefit of a written loan agreement with the husband's company in the period before the marriage. On relevant cohabitation, Bennett J noted at paragraph 55:

> "*Cohabitation, moving seamlessly into and beyond marriage, normally involves, in my judgment, a mutual commitment by two parties to make their lives together both in emotional and practical terms. Cohabitation is normally but not necessarily in one location. There is often a pooling of resources, both in money and property terms. Loans between cohabitants may be forgiven.*"

In ***N v F***[18], while there had been a period of premarital cohabitation, there was a nine-month period of separation and the breaking off of the parties' engagement before the parties' eventual marriage. On this basis Mostyn J was satisfied that the parties' cohabitation did not move "*seamlessly into marriage and did not 'extend the span of marriage de facto by reference to the premarital relationship*".

[17] *McCartney v Mills–McCartney* [2008] EWHC 401 (fam), [2008] 1 FLR 1508.

[18] [2011] EWHC 586 (Fam) [2011] 2 FLR 533.

2.2.3 Examples: where pre-martial cohabitation is included in the duration of the marriage

The court may find that the period of pre-marital relationship extends even before cohabitation, if the relationship is sufficiently committed. This was the case in ***J v J***[19], in which Bennett J considered that the parties' relationship commenced at the date of their engagement, the year before their cohabitation and 3.5 years before their eventual marriage. The relationship was found to have endured for just over 7 years in total, notwithstanding that the marriage was just 3.5 years.

In ***IX v IY***[20] Williams J considered the approach adopted in ***GW v RW***[21], (as well as other authorities), and concluded that premarital cohabitation should be treated as either extending the period of the marriage to create a marriage of longer duration, or, as a circumstance of the case, to be taken into account in a more general way. He explained that cohabitation prior to marriage is relevant because it may indicate that the parties had at that point entered into a partnership which may be indistinguishable from that which arises after marriage. At paragraph 68, Williams J described pre-marital cohabitation as where:

> "*prior to the formal commencement of marriage, the parties had entered into the sort of partnership involving the mutual support, working together, rights and obligations which may be indistinguishable from those which arise when parties begin to live together only after marriage*".

In the same paragraph he gave the following guidance:

> "*What the court must be looking to identify is a time at which the relationship had acquired sufficient mutuality of commitment to*

[19] [2004] EWHC 53 (Fam).

[20] [2018] EWHC 3053 (Fam), [2019] 2 FLR 449.

[21] [2003] EWHC 611 (Fam), [2003] 2 FLR 108.

> *equate to marriage. Of course, in very many cases, possibly most cases, this will be very obviously marked by the parties cohabiting, possibly in conjunction with the purchase of a property. However, in other cases, and this may be one of them, it is not so easy to identify. The mere fact that the parties begin to spend time in each other's homes does not of itself, it seems to me, equate to marriage. In situations such as this, the court must look to an accumulation of markers of marriage which eventually will take the relationship over the threshold into a quasi-marital relationship which may then either be added to the marriage to establish a longer marriage or which becomes a weightier factor as one of the circumstances of the case.*"

In that case, Williams J concluded that the parties' pre-marital relationship should be taken into account in the duration of the marriage because it was "*a committed relationship, which was moving towards marriage, in which children were contemplated and hoped for and in which the pattern of life which developed… continued largely without change, after the marriage took place*"[22].

2.2.4 *VV v VV* [2022] EWFC 41: recent guidance on the court's approach

In *VV v VV*[23], Peel J review this issue and noted at paragraph 44:

> "*… where cohabitation is in dispute, the court may need to inquire to an extent into the state of the relationship when evaluating the durability and permanence of the alleged cohabitation.*"

Peel J gave the following guidance as to what the court should look for when determining cohabitation disputes at paragraph 45:

---

22 [2003] EWHC 611 (Fam), [2003] 2 FLR 108. See paragraph 107(1).

23 [2022] EWFC 41, [2023] 1 FLR 170.

> "*... the court should also look at the parties' respective intentions when inquiring into cohabitation. Where one or both parties do not think they are in a quasi-marital arrangement, or are equivocal about it, that may weaken the cohabitation case. Where, by contrast, they both consider themselves to be in a quasi-marital arrangement, that is likely to strengthen the cohabitation case.*"

In ***VV v VV***[24], the relevance of the issue was whether assets accrued during the period of the parties' engagement and pre-marital cohabitation should be shared equally between the parties. The marriage had lasted for just five months, and the parties were in their fifties and had no children. The parties' became engaged in March 2019 and married in January 2020. The wife claimed that cohabitation began in November 2018, while the husband asserted that it started in December 2019. Peel J found that cohabitation does not require spending every night together under the same roof, particularly when a relationship straddles international boundaries. However, in this case, cohabitation did not commence until December 2019 when the husband left the USA permanently, and the parties moved into a London home together. Until then, they had been in a committed relationship where they spent time together, were supportive and affectionate towards each other, but which fell short of a quasi-martial relationship.

Peel J determined that the wife's sharing entitlement applied only during the period that he had found that they cohabited. Matrimonial property consists of everything acquired during the marriage (which should include periods of pre-marital cohabitation and engagement)[25]. While an engagement may be an indicator of the strength of the parties' commitment and shared life, it is not determinative of a sharing entitlement[26]. There is currently no reported authority where the fact of engagement generated a sharing entitlement, regardless of cohabitation.

---

[24] [2022] EWFC 41, [2023] 1 FLR 170.

[25] *Mille v Miller; McFarlane v McFarlane* [2006] UKHL 24.

[26] See *VV v VV* [2022] EWFC 41, [2023] 1 FLR 170, paragraph 48.

Therefore, although parties' engagement is a relevant factor when considering the parties' commitment and shared life, it did not by itself bring about a sharing entitlement. As the parties did not cohabit until after the husband acquired company shares, ceased employment and entered into a compromise agreement, the husband's shares were non-matrimonial and the wife was not entitled to share in them.

2.3 When does a marriage end?

In respect of the end of a marriage or civil partnership, the court will usually look at the date of separation, as opposed to the date of the final decree. However, it may be that although a marriage has broken down, the parties remain emotionally and financially enmeshed with one another. If this is the case, the court may consider it inappropriate to ignore the period post-separation during which the parties continue to be involved.

2.3.1 General guidance

In ***GW v RW***[27], Mr N Mostyn QC (as he then was, sitting as a Deputy High Court Judge) said that when assessing the duration of the marriage, the court has always looked at the position *de facto rather than de jure*. For example, the end of the marriage is always taken as the date of separation, rather than the date of the decree absolute. In ***GW v RW***, Mr Mostyn took the view that it would be unrealistic to include the 18-month period in which the parties were separated (with the wife petitioning for divorce and later withdrawing the petition) as part of the duration of the marriage.

27 [2003] EWHC 611 (Fam), [2003] 2 FLR 108.

The date of separation was of significance in ***WG v HG***[28], which was not a short marriage case, but contains important insight from Francis J regarding how the court should treat post marriage separation. The wife suffered a catastrophic brain injury following a horse-riding accident and made a good recovery but had ongoing needs arising from the accident. Before the accident, the parties had separated, with the husband presenting a divorce petition, but later reconciled, with the husband withdrawing the petition. The wife's position was that the parties remained reconciled at the time of her accident, and the husband's was that they had separated before the accident. The practical effect of this was the question of the husband's duty to meet the wife's post-accident needs. Francis J concluded at paragraph 34 that:

> *"As a matter of pure and obvious fact, the accident occurred during the marriage, the parties were not divorced. It occurred at a time that the parties knew that the marriage was more or less over but when the wife was still completely financially dependent on the husband. The husband properly met that obligation and has continued to do so, albeit under protest"*

He added at paragraph 35:

> *"If and insofar as the wife has a need arising from the accident, and if the husband is able to afford to meet that need, I am clear that he must do so. No one else is there to do so and there is no evidence at all that the wife would receive any state provision. I do not think in these cases it is possible to draw a line in the sand and say that if anything happens after a fixed point in time, it is nothing to do with the husband or this court. I have to make an order that is fair having regard to all of the circumstances of the case, and if I find that the wife has a financial need as a consequence of her accident, or indeed any other need, and if I find that the husband is able to meet it, then he should do so. Nor can I, in some artificial or arbitrary way, reduce the amount of support*

28 [2018] EWFC 84, [2018] All ER D 213.

that the husband should provide to the wife, on account of the fact that the marriage was almost over at the date of the accident."

In ***MB v EB***[29] the wife asserted that the marriage, which commenced in 2004, and was a short marriage, with the parties separating in 2004 when they stopped living together. The husband argued that the parties in fact separated in 2016, when he issued divorce proceedings. Cohen J considered that the approach outlined by Williams J in ***IX v IY***[30] for assessing the beginning of a marriage, can equally be applied to an attempt to define the date of the end of the marriage. The court's approach should be to consider when the relationship ceased to have "*sufficient mutuality of commitment to equate to marriage*". Cohen J noted, "*it is a truism that marriage comes in all different shapes and sizes. What may be important to one couple, may be trivial to another*"[31].

Cohen J found that the parties separated in 2004 because after 2004 they spent more time apart than they did together, the parties' met their own income needs while apart and, from 2005, the husband had other relationships and a separate home with neither party able to access the other's property. In addition, the parties executed a separation agreement in 2011 which stated that they had separated in 2004. However, Cohen J considered it inappropriate to disregard the entire period between 2004 to 2016 (when proceedings were brought) from all further consideration, acknowledging that neither party had moved on emotionally until after 2016.

---

29 [2019] EWHC 1649 2 FLR 899.

30 [2018] EWHC 3053 (Fam), [2019] 2 FLR 449.

31 paragraph 52.

2.3.2 Reconciliation post-divorce: *S v S (Financial Provision: Cohabitation after divorce)* [1994] 2 FLR 228

Reconciliation between parties' post-divorce may be approached in a similar way to premarital cohabitation as was established in ***S v S***. In ***S v S***, the parties began living together in 1963, married in 1969 and had two children. In 1976 the wife issued divorce proceedings, which culminated in decree absolute in 1977 followed by a consent order. The husband was to remain in the family home with the children until the youngest child attained the age of 18. Thereafter, the property was to be sold and the net proceeds divided equally between the parties. The husband was to pay £100 per month to the wife by way of periodical payments, but there was otherwise to be a clean break. During the Christmas period of 1977, the parties reconciled, and the wife returned to the family home. The property was sold in May 1978 and a new property purchased in the joint names of the parties. They continued to reside together until 1990 when the relationship finally broke down. In April 1992 the wife applied to set aside the consent order of 1977. In September 1992 she applied for leave to appeal out of time and sought an increase in the quantum of the periodical payments.

The court allowed the wife's appeal on the basis that there were new circumstances which invalidated the basis upon which the consent order was agreed, as per ***Barder v Caluori***[32]. The sale of the family home in 1978 made the order meaningless and unenforceable, and the resumption of cohabitation by the parties had undermined the fundamental assumptions which underpinned the consent order. In applying the s25 criteria the court was obliged to regard the periods of cohabitation separately from the period of eight years in which the parties were married. In this case the court gave considerable weight to the role the wife had played throughout the course of the relationship, including post-marital cohabitation, over circa 29 years, in being a mother to the

[32] *Barder v Caluori* [1988] AC 20.

children, running the family home and supporting the husband in his career. There was therefore to be a clean break along the ***Duxbury*** lines.

2.3.3 Post-separation delay: *Butler v Butler* [2023] EWFC 2453

Butler v Butler is an example of a case where the court found that the parties' marriage effectively lasted six years although divorce proceedings were not started until several years later. After they separated, the parties were found to have remained married in name only. Moor J dismissed the wife's appeal in financial remedy proceedings where the judge had made an order that did not meet her housing needs because there were insufficient assets to do so. The parties lived together only briefly. The wife was based in Birmingham until 2007, when she moved to East London, and she rented separate accommodation from then on. The husband also lived in East London. He inherited a tenanted property from his father in 2007. He eventually sold the property in 2015. With the sale proceeds, he purchased a house. At the final hearing, the main issue was the parties' housing needs. In terms of income, the parties had been financially independent of each other for several years. The wife sought the sale of the husband's house and £300,000 to rehouse herself, and their two children in a three-bedroom property in East London.

Recorder Anderson found that the husband's property was non-matrimonial in nature. He considered that the order the wife sought would result in the husband becoming homeless. He ordered the husband to pay a lump sum of £58,000 on a clean break basis, which the husband could raise by equity release. Moor J dismissed the wife's subsequent appeal. He found that Recorder Anderson was entitled to make the order and the husband's non-matrimonial property should not be invaded further.

Moor J's judgment is a reminder that where a judge concludes that a case is a needs case, this does not mean that they must make an order that satisfies both parties' needs. In many cases, there are sufficient assets to meet the parties' needs and that is the right outcome, even if it means invading non-matrimonial property. However, this case fell into a different category where the assets were insufficient to meet both parties' needs.

CHAPTER THREE

NEEDS IN A SHORT MARRIAGE CASE

3.1 What are needs?

In ***Miller v Miller; McFarlane v McFarlane***[33], Lord Nicholls and Baroness Hale made clear that needs are assessed by reference to a wide variety of factors including the parties' ages, their future earning capacity, the family's standard of living and any disability of either party.

Judges have a broad discretion available to them when it comes to assessment of needs, particularly in short marriage cases. In ***FF v KF***[34], Mostyn J said:

> *"So far as the "needs" principle is concerned there is an almost unbounded discretion. The main rule is that, save in a situation of real hardship, the "needs" must be causally related to the marriage. Like equity in the old days, the result seems to depend on the length of the judge's foot. It is worth recalling that Heather Mills-McCartney was awarded over £25m to meet her "needs" (McCartney v McCartney [2008] EWHC 401 (Fam), [2008] 1 FLR 1508). Mrs Juffali was awarded £62m to meet her 'needs' (Juffali v Juffali [2016] EWHC 1684 (Fam), [2017] 1 FLR 729). In the very recent case of AAZ v BBZ [2016] EWHC 3234 (Fam) the court assessed the applicant-wife's "needs" in the remarkable sum of £224m. Plainly "needs" does not mean needs. It is a term of art. Obviously, no-one actually needs £25m, or £62m, or £224m for accommodation and sustenance. The main drivers in the discretionary exercise are the scale*

33 [2006] UKHL 24, [2006] 2 AC 618, paragraph 11.

34 [2017] EWHC 1093, paragraph 18.

> *of the payer's wealth, the length of the marriage, the applicant's age and health, and the standard of living, although the latter factor cannot be allowed to dominate the exercise.*
>
> *In a short marriage case the discretion when assessing needs is particularly broad and fact-sensitive....*"

In short marriage cases, the focus of the court's needs assessment has been to enable the financially-weaker party to transition from the marriage to independent living. In ***Miller; McFarlane***[35], on the principles of needs and compensation, Baroness Hale said, "*the ultimate objective is to give each party an equal start on the road to independent living.*"

In ***H v H***[36], Charles J stated:

> "*The provision awarded should enable a gentle transition for the party who made the domestic contribution from the standard of living enjoyed during the marriage to the standard that she could expect as a self-sufficient woman...and in my view the length of the marriage and the role of an ex-wife as the primary caretaker of the children of the marriage would be factors to be taken into account in determining the amount of the provision to meet that transition.*"

An example of an award made for the purpose of enabling the financially weaker party to transition to independent living in a big-money short marriage case is ***VV v VV***[37]. In *VV*, the marriage was 7 months in length, the husband had significant wealth and the wife minimal assets and earning capacity. The wife was awarded £60,000 to discharge her mortgage, £237,000 to clear her liabilities and capitalised maintenance of £450,000 to cover 3 years of 'rehabilitative maintenance'.

---

35 [2006] UKHL 24, [2006] 2 AC 618, paragraph 144.

36 [2007] EWHC 459 (Fam), [2007] 2 FLR 548, paragraph 96.

37 [2022] EWFC 41, [2023] 1 FLR 170.

An example of an award for transition-based needs in a modest assets case is ***D v D (Financial Remedy Case)***[38], in which District Judge John Smart considered a case following 10-month marriage. The assets were the former matrimonial home, which had been brought into the marriage by the husband, and the husband's pension. The husband had two adult children and the wife had a son living independently. The court ordered that the wife should receive 21% of the net assets (excluding pensions) in order to rehouse herself in rented accommodation and discharge her debts. The order meant that the husband may need to sell the former matrimonial depending on his mortgage capacity. The husband was also ordered to pay periodical payments to the wife for 2 years.

This chapter will consider the following questions in the context of short marriages:

- When do needs take precedence over sharing?
- What is the relevance of the standard of living during the marriage to the needs assessment?
- Must needs be generated by the marriage?
- How do children impact on needs?
- Is non-matrimonial property relevant to needs?

3.2 When do needs take precedence over sharing?

In ***Miller; McFarlane***[39], Baroness Hale confirmed that the order in which the principles of needs, sharing and compensation are considered will

---

[38] [2020] EWFC B24.

[39] [2006] UKHL 24, [2006] 2 AC 618.

depend on the facts of each case, there not being a hard and fast rule about whether one starts with sharing or needs.

Generally, the financially weaker party will be awarded the higher of an award based on sharing or needs. In ***FF v KF***[40], Mostyn J explained:

> "*The authorities make clear, and common sense dictates, that the result is the higher of the two figures generated by the principles. So, if the sharing principle produces a figure of £1 million but the needs principle produces a figure of £4 million then the result is £4 million. Equivalently, if the needs principle produces a figure of £1 million but the sharing principle produces a figure of £4 million then the result, again, is £4 million. There is no warrant for suggesting, when one has arrived at the higher of the two figures generated by the principles, that one can augment it by further unspecified factors...*"

In the vast majority of cases the court's exercise will begin and end at the needs stage. Often, this will be because there are insufficient assets available to meet both parties' needs, and the court prioritises the meeting of needs over sharing. As Lord Nicholls put it in ***Miller; McFarlane***[41]:

> "*In most cases the search for fairness largely begins and ends at this stage. In most cases the available assets are insufficient to provide adequately for the needs of two homes. The court seeks to stretch modest finite resources so far as possible to meet the parties' needs.*"

In short marriage cases, it is more likely that a party's needs claim will subsume their sharing claim than in longer marriage cases. This is because in short marriages there will have been less time for the generation of marital assets than in longer marriages, and the financially-weaker party's needs are likely to be greater than their share of the marital acquest.

40 [2017] EWHC 1093, paragraph 17.

41 [2006] UKHL 24, [2006] 2 AC 618, paragraph 62.

This point is illustrated in the case of ***McCartney v Mills McCartney***[42], where Heather Mills was awarded £16.5m to meet her needs, that figure being higher than half of the matrimonial assets in circumstances where the vast majority of Paul McCartney's £400m work of assets had been accrued before the marriage.

Similarly, in ***FF v KF***[43] the total assets, most of which were pre-matrimonial, were £37m, and the marital acquest some £2m. The wife's needs award of £4.25m was higher than her sharing claim of £1m and Mostyn J upheld the £4.25m award on appeal.

As sharing awards will be smaller in short marriage cases than long marriage cases by virtue of the fact that there has been less time to accumulate matrimonial property, and needs take priority over sharing, it follows that in the vast majority of short marriage cases, the financially-weaker party's needs-based award will be higher than their sharing award, and the needs award will prevail. However, there will be short marriage cases where the sharing award is greater than the needs award. Whether the needs or sharing award is higher, the courts will need to ensure that any award made provides for fairness between the parties when cross-checked against a percentage division of the net assets.

3.3 Assessment of Needs: Standard of living during the marriage

The standard of living enjoyed by the parties during the marriage is one of the statutory factors which must be taken into account by the court in every financial remedies case[44]. The case law makes clear that the standard of living enjoyed during the marriage is less relevant to the assessment of the financially-weaker party's needs following a short marriage than a

42 [2008] EWHC 401 (Fam), [2008] 1 FLR 1508.

43 [2017] EWHC 1093.

44 Matrimonial Causes Act 1973 s 25(2)(c).

long marriage, and that needs may therefore be assessed more conservatively following a short marriage than a long marriage.

In ***Miller; McFarlane***[45], Baroness Hale established that the parties' standard of living during the marriage is the benchmark by which needs should be assessed, noting that the court's aim is to ensure the parties and their children have enough to supply their needs at the level as close as possible to that enjoyed during the marriage.

The length of the marriage is relevant when the court considers how much time the parties have had to become accustomed to the standard of living of the marriage. Where the parties have spent less time becoming accustomed to the marital standard of living, the standard of living will be less relevant to an assessment of their needs than it would be following a longer marriage.

In ***G v G***[46], when summarising the guidance on the application of the statutory principles, Charles J said:

> "*(b) the length of the marriage is relevant to determining the period for which that level of lifestyle is to be enjoyed by the payee (so long as this is affordable by the payor), and so also, if there is to be a return to a lesser standard of living for the payee, the period over which that transition should take place*
>
> *(c) if the marriage is short, this supports the conclusion that the award should be directed to providing a transition over an appropriate period for the payee spouse to either a lower long term standard of living than that enjoyed during the marriage, or to one that is not contributed to by the other spouse*".

Later in his judgment, Charles J explained that after an appropriate period of adjustment, that period being determined by reference to the

45 [2006] UKHL 24, [2006] 2 AC 618, paragraph 138.

46 [2012] EWHC 167 (Fam), [2012] 2 FLR 48, paragraph 136.

duration of the marriage, the standard of living enjoyed during the marriage is not the appropriate benchmark for the independent lifestyles of the parties[47].

In ***Miller; McFarlane***[48], Lord Nicholls was careful to restrict the scope of the court's assessment of the standard of living enjoyed during the marriage. In particular, the court is not required to consider one parties' hopes for the future based on the wealth of the person they have married. Lord Nicolls stated at paragraph 58:

> "*No doubt both parties had high hopes for their future when they married. But hopes and expectations, as such, are not an appropriate basis on which to assess financial needs. Claims for expectation losses do not fit altogether comfortably with the notion that each party is free to end the marriage. Indeed, to make an award by reference to the parties' future expectations would come close to restoring the 'tailpiece' which was originally part of s 25 of the 1973 Act. By that tailpiece the court was required to place the parties, so far as practical and, having regard to their conduct, just to do so, in the same financial position as they would have been had the marriage not broken down. It would be a mistake indirectly to re-introduce the effect of that discredited provision.*"

In ***McCartney v Mills McCartney***[49], Bennett J was clear that the needs of the financially-weaker party following a short marriage should be assessed more conservatively than following a long a marriage. Notably, the financially-weaker party cannot expect to continue to enjoy the standard of living they enjoyed during the short marriage for the rest of their life (see paragraphs 214 and 240).

47 Ibid. paragraph 200.

48 [2006] UKHL 24, [2006] 2 AC 618.

49 [2008] EWHC 401 (Fam), [2008] 1 FLR 1508.

In ***E v L***[50], on considering the wife's housing needs following a marriage of just four years, Mostyn J said:

> "*On payment of the lump sum the wife will be left with £1.59m outside her home in West London. That flat has been her home for many years. I do not accept that after a marriage of this brief duration needs have been generated which entitle her to a significant upgrade in her accommodation. She and her dog had lived there happily for years before the husband came into her life.* ***I agree with Mr Webster that the teaching of the authorities is that the duration of the marriage impacts forcefully and directly on the assessment of need.*** *The wife's stated ambition to achieve a significantly better accommodation is not a reasonable need after a marriage of this short duration.*" (emphasis added)

In ***Helliwell v Entwistle***[51], which concerned a three year marriage, Francis J upheld a pre-nuptial agreement which prevented sharing and limited the husband's award to his reasonable needs. He considered the husband's needs budget had been grossly inflated: even if the parties had spent large amounts on flights and meals during the marriage, that did not elevate the needs of the financially weaker party at the conclusion of the marriage. Francis J said at paragraph 140:

> "*Being married to a rich person for three years does not suddenly catapult you into a right to live like that for very (sic.) after the relationship has ended.*"

An example of a short marriage case in which the court assessed the wife's needs conservatively, by reference to the standard of living during the marriage is ***AB v FC***[52]. In that case Roberts J considered a marriage of

50 *(Financial Remedies)* [2021] EWFC 60, [2022] 1 FLR 952, paragraph 102.

51 [2024] EWHC 740 (Fam).

52 [2016] EWHC 3258 (Fam).

just 19 months, where the husband was a professional footballer. The parties had lived in luxurious rented accommodation during the marriage and had no assets other than a house in Miami in the husband's name worth just under £1m. The wife sought a budget to enable her to purchase a property for her and the child of the family worth £1.1m (comparable to the former matrimonial home) and £318,000 per annum in global maintenance.

Roberts J said at paragraph 77:

> *"It has to be borne carefully in mind that there is an inter-relationship between the level at which future needs will be assessed and the period during which a court is likely to find those needs should be met by the paying former spouse. The longer the period, the more likely it is that the court will decline to assess those needs on the basis of a standard of living which replicates that enjoyed during the marriage."*

Roberts J concluded that the wife's needs were for purchased accommodation as opposed to rented, but that the standard of property she needed was lower than the former matrimonial home. The husband was ordered to sell the Miami property and pay 36% of the proceeds or £270,000 from the proceeds (whichever is greater) to the wife, in order to enable her to purchase a property worth £700,000. The husband was ordered to pay the wife a mortgage allowance of £80,000 per annum and maintenance for her and their child of £120,000 per annum for at least the next 7 years. The husband was also ordered to pay school fees for the child of the marriage and discharge the wife's outstanding liabilities of £127,500.

Note that the court's power to assess needs more conservatively following a short marriage than a longer marriage is subject to the needs any children of the marriage, and in particular the need to house any children of the marriage with their primary carer[53]. See section 3.5 on children below for more detail.

3.4 Assessment of Needs: Needs generated by the marriage

There will have been less time during a short marriage for needs to be generated than in a long marriage, which may well impact on the needs assessment of the financially-weaker party.

There is some dispute within the judiciary as to whether the needs justifying a party's award must be causally connected to the marriage itself. In ***SS v NS***[54], Mostyn J said:

> "*Pulling the threads together it seems to me that the relevant principles in play on an application for spousal maintenance are as follows:*
>
> *(i) A spousal maintenance award is properly made where the evidence shows that choices made during the marriage have generated hard future needs on the part of the claimant. Here the duration of the marriage and the presence of children are pivotal factors.*
>
> ...
>
> *(iii) Where the needs in question are not causally connected to the marriage the award should generally be aimed at alleviating significant hardship...*"

In ***FF v KF***[55] Mostyn J repeated his view that save in a situation of real hardship, the "needs" must be causally related to the marriage. ***FF v KF***[56]

[53] see *JL v NN* [2024] EWHC 1489 (Fam).

[54] *(Spousal Maintenance)* [2014] EWHC 4183, paragraph 46.

[55] [2017] EWHC 1093, paragraph 18.

[56] Ibid.

concerned a marriage of just 4.5 years, following which the wife suffered a serious psychological breakdown as a result of the marriage, which affected her earning capacity, and was a relevant factor when assessing her needs.

However, in ***ND v GD***[57], Peel J was clear that a needs assessment must incorporate needs arising from the parties' physical health and disabilities, even if they had been generated outside of the marriage. He said at paragraphs 49-50:

> "*[49] Needs are an elastic concept. They cannot be looked at in isolation. In Charman v Charman (No 4) [2007] EWCA Civ 503, [2007] 1 FLR 1246, at para [70], the court said: 'The principle of need requires consideration of the financial needs, obligations and responsibilities of the parties (s 25(2)(b)); of the standard of living enjoyed by the family before the breakdown of the marriage (s 25(2)(c)); of the age of each party (half of s 25(2)(d)); and of any physical or mental disability of either of them (s 25(2)(e)).'...*
>
> *[50] Counsel for H submits that needs should be 'relationship-generated'. The logic, in its purest form, is that W's health is not causally linked to the marriage, was diagnosed after separation and therefore none of her needs occasioned by health fall to be met by H. He shied away from pressing me to reach this conclusion, but invited me to bear this in mind when considering needs in the round. In my judgment, this approach cannot be right. The statute does not limit consideration of needs in this way (s 25(2)(e)). In Miller v Miller; McFarlane v McFarlane [2006] UKHL 24, [2006] 2 AC 618, [2006] 1 FLR 1186, at para [11], Lord Nicholls of Birkenhead said: 'Most of these needs will have been generated by the marriage, but not all of them. Needs arising from age or disability are instances of the latter*".

[57] *(Financial Remedies)* [2021] EWFC 53, [2022] 1 FLR 716.

It is noted that the dictum of Mostyn J and Peel J is not entirely inconsistent. In ***SS v NS***[58], Mostyn J leaves space for the court to consider needs not generated by the marriage, if, to do otherwise would cause a situation of 'real hardship'. Serious disability or health issues affecting a party's ability to work and/or necessitating additional care would plainly risk leaving a party in a situation of real hardship if not addressed. It seems therefore that there is certainly room for the court to consider needs arising other than from the marriage in a needs assessment, particularly where doing so would risk causing hardship.

It's clear that judges have a huge amount of discretion when it comes to interpreting a parties' needs requirement, and how those needs relate to the marriage, particularly in short marriage cases. As Mostyn J said in ***FF v KF***[59]:

> "*In a short marriage case the discretion when assessing needs is particularly broad and fact-sensitive….*"

The broad discretion available to family judges is evident in the case law, which includes examples of both broad and narrow needs assessments in cases of short marriages. An example of a narrow needs assessment is ***WD v MH***[60]. Examples of very broad needs assessments after short to medium marriages are ***M v L***[61] and ***S v S***[62].

In ***WD v MH***[63], Recorder Rhys Taylor considered that the wife was able to meet her needs without recourse to the husband's funds in

58 *(Spousal Maintenance)* [2014] EWHC 4183.

59 [2017] EWHC 1093.

60 [2022] EWFC 162 (B).

61 *(Financial Relied After Overseas Divorce)* [2003] EWHC 328 (Fam), [2003] 2 FLR 425.

62 [2008] EWHC 519 (Fam), [2008] 2 FLR 113.

63 [2022] EWFC 162 (B).

circumstances where her needs were conservatively met by her living in a council property and claiming benefits. The magnetic factors in that case were the shortness of the marriage, an agreement reached between the parties in 2008 and the wife's delay in bringing an application for financial remedies. Recorder Taylor stated at paragraph 73dii:

> "*Needs are an elastic concept and I am entitled to bear in mind the shortness of the marriage when considering what needs are casually related to a relationship.*"

M v L[64] concerned a 4 year marriage following which the wife delayed for 30 years after separation before she brought her Part III application. The court was satisfied that the wife remained dependent on the husband even 30 years after separation as a result of the children of the marriage and the husband's continued voluntary maintenance contributions since separation. The court declined to replicate the standard of living during the marriage or to divide the husband's capital, but considered it was plainly fair to award the wife capitalised maintenance of £150,000 (£1,000 per month for 12.5 years) and half the proceeds of the former matrimonial home, in circumstances where the husband was very wealthy and had the means to pay.

In ***S v S***[65] Mark Potter P considered an appeal following a medium term marriage of 11 years. The court was satisfied that the wife needed a property large enough for her horses, because her love of horses during the marriage had been a prominent feature of the parties' lives and was a relevant factor. Further, the court considered the wife's budget of £81,300 per annum reasonable considering the high standard of living during the marriage and the budget submitted by the husband. Note that

---

64 *(Financial Relied After Overseas Divorce)* [2003] EWHC 328 (Fam), [2003] 2 FLR 425.

65 [2008] EWHC 519 (Fam).

there were sufficient funds to enable the husband to live comfortably while providing extravagantly for the wife's needs.

3.5 Assessment of Needs: Children

The most obvious and common need generated by a marriage will be the presence of children of the family, who need to be housed and maintained. The welfare of any minor child or children will be the first consideration of the court[66]. In almost every case of a short marriage, the needs related to the presence of a child will take precedence over the fact that the marriage was short. Children have the capacity to change everything when it comes to the assessment of needs.

There are examples of the court making provision for spousal maintenance over a significant period due to the presence of children. For example in ***C v C***[67], which concerned a marriage of just 9.5 months, ***R v R***[68] which concerned a 7-year marriage, ***G v G***[69], which concerned a 5-year marriage, and ***X v D***[70], which concerned a marriage of just four months.

There is certainly precedent for the court rejecting the argument that a parent-spouse should not be entitled to outright housing provision after a short marriage:

---

66 Matrimonial Causes Act 1973 s 25(1).

67 *(financial relief: short marriage)* [1997] 2 FLR 26.

68 *(Financial Remedies: Needs and Practicalities)* [2011] EWHC 3093, [2013] 1 FLR 120.

69 [2012] EWHC 167 (Fam), [2012] 2 FLR 48.

70 [2023] EWFC 332 (B)

- In ***B v B***[71], a case in which the marriage lasted less than one year, the husband was ordered to pay the wife a lump sum of £175,000 to enable her to purchase a house and the husband's argument that any property purchased for the benefit of the wife and the child should be held on the terms of a *Mesher* order was rejected at first instance and on appeal.

- In ***X v D***[72], in which the parties were married for just four months but had one child together, the court rejected the husband's submission that his company could purchase a property to be used by the wife until their child was 21. Moreover, while neither party argued for a *Mesher* (at least initially) the court considered the arguments and agreed that one would be inappropriate in the circumstances of the case.

- In ***UD v TQ***[73], where the marriage had been very short with the parties' hardly living together at all, His Honour Judge Hess rejected the husband's argument that he should retain an interest in the apartment where the wife was living with the parties' 3 year old child.

The court's practice of making significant maintenance orders and outright housing provision in short marriage cases in which there are children is explained by Holman J in ***Murphy v Murphy***[74]. He said at paragraph 35:

> "*What, frankly, the arguments by the husband overlook is that the having of children changes everything. Of course this wife could never have expected a "meal ticket for life" on the basis of six years of marriage*

[71] *(Mesher Order)*[2002] EWHC 3106 (Fam), [2003] 2 FLR 285.

[72] [2023] EWFC 332 (B)

[73] [2024] EWFC 119 (B).

[74] [2014] EWHC 2263, paragraph 35.

and two years of cohabitation if there had been no children. Far from it, she would no doubt have continued to work at Selfridges, or in similar employment, and at the point of the breakdown of their marriage and divorce there would have been a fair capital division and a clean break and each would have gone their own way. But the fact of having children, and their obvious dependence in this particular case on their mother for their care, changes everything, as I have said. The economic impact on this wife is likely to endure not only until they leave school but, indeed, for the rest of her life."

3.6 Non-matrimonial property and needs

In the vast majority of cases, the court's enquiry will begin and end with the parties' needs. It is only in those cases where there is a surplus of assets over needs that the sharing principle is engaged. Non-matrimonial property is far less relevant in needs cases than sharing cases as needs take priority over sharing and the court is able to invade non-matrimonial property in order to meet needs.

The prioritisation of needs over non-matrimonial property applies equally in short marriage cases as long marriage cases. In ***M-D v D-D***[75], Sir Mark Potter P allowed an appeal from an order which failed to adequately meet the wife's needs after a 5-year marriage as a result of the District Judge placing too much weight on the husband's pre-acquired property and inadequate weight on the wife's needs, particularly her need to build up her pension provision.

However, it has been suggested that non-matrimonial property may be relevant to an assessment of needs. In ***N v F***[76] Mostyn J considered that the assessment of needs was not an insulated metric uninformed by factors that are key to the performance of the sharing principle. Needs

75 [2008] EWHC 1929 (Fam), [2009] 1 FLR 810.

76 [2011] EWHC 586, [2011] 2 FLR 522.

are assessed by reference to the available wealth and the marital standard of living (as in ***McCartney v Mills McCartney***[77]), and to the terms of pre-nuptial agreements (***Radmacher (formerly Granatino) v Granatino***[78]). Mostyn J leaves open the possibly that needs may also be assessed by reference to non-matrimonial property, noting at paragraph 19:

> *"So if an agreement to preserve non-matrimonial property can have the effect of assessing need more conservatively (indeed in Granatino far more conservatively) than would have been the case absent that factor, why cannot the presence of pre-marital property simpliciter not have an equivalent or similar effect?"*

In ***WC v HC***[79], Peel J said:

> *"... As Mostyn J said in **FF v KF [2017] EWHC 1093** at [18];*
>
> > *"The main drivers in the discretionary exercise are the scale of the payer's wealth, the length of the marriage, the applicant's age and health, and the standard of living, although the latter factor cannot be allowed to dominate the exercise".*
>
> *I would add that **the source of the wealth is also relevant to needs.** If it is substantially non-marital, then in my judgment it would be unfair not to weigh that factor in the balance. Mostyn J made a similar observation in **N v F [2011] 2 FLR 533** at [17-19]"* (emphasis added).

77 [2008] EWHC 401 (Fam), [2008] 1 FLR 1508.

78 [2010] UKSC 42, [2011] 1 AC 534.

79 [2022] EWFC 22, [2022] WLR 65, paragraph 21 (xv).

Note that neither ***N v F***[80] nor ***WC v HC***[81] were short marriage cases, but the guidance of Mostyn J and Peel J will be as applicable to short marriage cases as long ones.

In ***Butler v Butler***[82], the only available property was a non-matrimonial property purchased by the husband 9 years after his separation from the wife following their 6 year marriage. The wife had always lived in local authority accommodation. At first instance, the husband was ordered to pay the wife a lump sum of £58,000 (the property was worth £400,000). The wife appealed on the basis that the award did not meet her needs. Considering the appeal, Moor J made clear that the judge's order could not be criticised in circumstances where there are insufficient assets to meet both parties' needs. If the husband's property were sold, and any more paid to the wife than £58,000, then the husband would have nowhere to live, and would not have enabled the wife to re-house.

For analysis of non-matrimonial property in relation to the sharing principle, please see below.

---

80 [2011] EWHC 586, [2011] 2 FLR 522.

81 [2022] EWFC 22, [2022] WLR 65.

82 [2023] EWHC 2453 (Fam)

CHAPTER FOUR

SHARING IN A SHORT MARRIAGE CASE

4.1 What is sharing?

The sharing principle was introduced in ***White v White***[83] and affirmed and expanded upon in ***Miller v Miller, McFarlane v McFarlane***[84]. The principle is that the fruits of the marriage (matrimonial or family assets) should be shared equally between the parties, regardless of the nature of their contributions during the marriage.

The principle of equal sharing applies just as much to short marriages as to long marriages. In ***Miller; McFarlane***[85] Lord Nicholls said:

> "*[16] A third strand is sharing. This 'equal sharing' principle derives from the basic concept of equality permeating a marriage as understood today. Marriage, it is often said, is a partnership of equals. In 1992 Lord Keith of Kinkel approved Lord Emslie's observation that 'husband and wife are now for all practical purposes equal partners in marriage': R v R [1992] 1 AC 599, 617. This is now recognised widely, if not universally. The parties commit themselves to sharing their lives. They live and work together. When their partnership ends each is entitled to an equal share of the assets of the partnership, unless there is a good reason to the contrary. Fairness requires no less. But I emphasise the qualifying phrase: 'unless there is good reason to the*

83 [2000] UKHL 54, [2001] AC 596.

84 [2006] UKHL 24, [2006] 2 AC 618.

85 Ibid. paragraphs 16-17.

contrary'. The yardstick of equality is to be applied as an aid, not a rule.

*[17] **This principle is applicable as much to short marriages as to long marriages:** see Foster v Foster [2003] EWCA Civ 565; [2003] 2 FLR 299, 305, para 19 per Hale LJ. A short marriage is no less a partnership of equals than a long marriage. The difference is that a short marriage has been less enduring. In the nature of things this will affect the quantum of the financial fruits of the partnership."*

Subsequent case law has affirmed that the sharing principle applies equally to short marriage cases as long marriage cases. In ***E v L***[86], the husband argued that due to the short 4-year length of the marriage and there being no children, the equal sharing principle should not apply to the matrimonial acquest. Mostyn J made clear that the equal sharing principle applies uniformly across all marriages, regardless of the age of the parties, the length of the marriage, or whether the parties have children or not. In relation to the length of the marriage, Mostyn J made clear that there is no logical reason to draw a distinction between an accrual over a short period and an accrual over a long period. The impact of the duration of the marriage on sharing would be reflected by the fact that in a short marriage there will have been less time for accrual than in a longer marriage.

Note that the sharing principle will only be engaged in cases where both parties needs are met and there is a surplus of assets available to be shared. The vast majority of cases will begin and end at the needs stage.

The court's approach to the equal sharing principle is first to assess the quantum of the "matrimonial assets" and the "non-matrimonial assets", and secondly to consider whether the principle of equal sharing should be departed from in order to meet needs or in recognition of unmatched contributions. The most complicated part of the sharing process is

86 *(Financial Remedies)* [2021] EWFC 60, [2022] 1 FLR 952.

assessing what is and is not matrimonial property, whether contributions should impact on equal sharing of matrimonial property, and to what extent any non-matrimonial property should be excluded from the sharing principle.

This chapter will consider the following issues, particularly in relation to short marriages:

- Matrimonial assets
- Non-matrimonial assets and the court's approach to them
- Unilateral assets
- Unmatched contributions

4.2 Non-matrimonial property

4.2.1 What are matrimonial assets?

Matrimonial or family assets are the assets of the marriage which are ripe for equal sharing under the sharing principle.

In ***Miller; McFarlane***[87], Baroness Hale gave the following examples of family assets:

> *"Prime examples of family assets of a capital nature were the family home and its contents, while the parties' earning capacities were assets of a revenue nature. But also included are other assets which were obviously acquired for the use and benefit of the whole family, such as holiday homes, caravans, furniture, insurance policies and other family savings. To this list should clearly be added family businesses or joint ventures in which they both work. It is easy to see such assets as the*

87 [2006] UKHL 24, [2006] 2 AC 618, paragraph 149

> *fruits of the marital partnership. It is also easy to see each party's efforts as making a real contribution to the acquisition of such assets."*

In ***JL v SL***[88] Mostyn J described matrimonial property as "*the property which the parties have built up by their joint (but inevitably different) efforts during the span of their partnership*".

4.2.2 What is non-matrimonial property?

Non-matrimonial property can be accrued before, during or after the marriage. Examples of non-matrimonial property include:

- Wealth/property brought into the marriage[89].

- Trust assets acquired before the marriage[90].

- Inheritance monies received by one party[91].

- Inheritance property received by one party e.g. farm, ancestral castle[92].

---

88 *(No2) (Appeal: Non-Matrimonial Property)* [2015] EWHC 360 (Fam), [2015] 2 FLR 1202, paragraph 18.

e.g. *McCartney v Mills-McCartney* [2008] EWHC 401 (Fam), [2008] 1 FLR 1508.

90 e.g. *WX v HX (Treatment of matrimonial and non-matrimonial property)* [2021] EWHC 241 (Fam).

91 e.g. *Norris v Norris* [2002] EWHC 2996 (Fam), [2003] 1 FLR 1142.

92 e.g. *Robson v Robson* [2010] EWCA Civ 1171, [2011] 1 FLR 751.

- Inherited shares received by one party[93].

- Share options acquired before the marriage[94].

- Companies started before the marriage[95].

- Properties purchased post-separation with funds generated post-separation[96].

- Income received post-separation[97].

- Proceeds from the sale of business assets sold post-separation[98].

- Bonuses received more than 12 months after separation[99].

- Lottery winnings received during the marriage where the lottery ticket was purchased by one party using their own earnings[100].

---

93 e.g. *K v L (Non-Matrimonial Property: Special Contribution)* [2011] EWCA Civ 550, [2011] 2 FLR 980.

94 e.g. *VV v VV* [2023] EWFC 41, [2023] 1 FLR 170.

95 e.g. *Jones v Jones* [2011] EWCA Civ 41, [2011] 1 FLR 1723.

96 *Rossi v Rossi* [2006] EWHC 1482 (Fam), [2007] 1 FLR 790.

97 e.g. *E v L (Financial Remedies)* [2021] EWFC 60, [2022] 1 FLR 952; *B v B* [2010] EWHC 193 (Fam), [2010] 2 FLR 1214.

98 e.g. *JL v SL (No 2) (Appeal: Non-Matrimonial Property)* [2015] EWHC 360 (Fam), [2015] 2 FLR 1202.

99 e.g. *Rossi v Rossi* [2006] EWHC 1482 (Fam), [2007] 1 FLR 790.

100 e.g. *S v AG (Financial Orders: Lottery Prize)* [2011] EWHC 2637 (Fam), [2012] 1 FLR 651.

- Passive growth on non-matrimonial assets[101].

4.2.3 How does the court approach non-matrimonial property?

Unless non-matrimonial property is needed to meet the parties' needs, it will be excluded from the matrimonial pot before the contents of the pot are shared equally between the spouses, remaining the property of the spouse to whom it belongs.

In ***Miller; McFarlane***[102], Lord Nicholls made clear that non-matrimonial property is more likely to be excluded from equal sharing in cases of short marriages:

> "*[23] The matter stands differently regarding property ('non-matrimonial property') the parties bring with them into the marriage or acquire by inheritance or gift during the marriage. Then the duration of the marriage will be highly relevant. …*
>
> *[24] In the case of a short marriage fairness may well require that the claimant should not be entitled to a share of the other's non-matrimonial property. The source of the asset may be a good reason for departing from equality. This reflects the instinctive feeling that parties will generally have less call upon each other on the breakdown of a short marriage.*"

Non-matrimonial property is more relevant in short marriages than longer marriages. Within short marriages there will have been less time for non-matrimonial assets to become mixed and mingled with matrimonial assets, meaning that the non-matrimonial source of the asset

---

101 e.g. *Rossi v Rossi* [2006] EWHC 1482 (Fam), [2007] 1 FLR 790; *Jones v Jones* [2011] EWCA Civ 41, [2011] 1 FLR 1723.

102 [2006] UKHL 24, [2006] 2 AC 618, paragraphs 23-24

remains relevant. This is acknowledged by Baroness Hale in ***Miller; McFarlane***[103]:

> "*In the White case, it was also recognised that the importance of the source of the assets will diminish over time. As the family's personal and financial interdependence grows, it becomes harder and harder to disentangle what came from where.*" (paragraph 148)
>
> "*The source of the assets may be taken into account but its importance will diminish over time. Put the other way round, the court is expressly required to take into account the duration of the marriage: section 25(2)(d). If the assets are not "family assets", or not generated by the joint efforts of the parties, then the duration of the marriage may justify a departure from the yardstick of equality of division.*" (paragraph 152)

Pre-acquired assets are more likely to maintain their status as 'wholly non-matrimonial' following a short marriage than a long one. This point is illustrated by Mostyn J in ***Rossi v Rossi***[104]:

> "*The court will decide whether it should be shared and if so in what proportions. In so deciding it will have regard to the reality that the longer the marriage the more likely non-matrimonial property will become merged or entangled with matrimonial property. By contrast, in a short marriage case non-matrimonial assets are not likely to be shared unless needs require this.*"

In ***H v H***[105], Singer J considered a relatively short marriage, where the parties had cohabited for 7 years but been married for less than 2 years. Singer J expressed the view that subject to needs requirements, fairness may dictate that assets derived from pre-marriage acquisition or gift

---

103 Ibid.

104 [2006] EWHC 1482 (Fam), [2007] 1 FLR 790 at paragraph 24.

105 *(financial provision)* [2009] EWHC 494 (Fam), [2009] 2 FLR 795.

should be wholly or partially left out of the dividing exercise. It was however an important part of the exercise as to whether the relevant assets had been kept wholly separate and apart or had been used for family purposes, such as the parties' matrimonial home. Singer J said at paragraph 78:

> "*there is a world of difference between the approach to be adopted to (for instance) a pre-marriage property which has been the parties' matrimonial home; and a gifted or inherited fund kept separate from and never mingled with the matrimonial budget; and a gift or inheritance fully deployed and utilised for family purposes and needs.*"

Whilst it is clear that the presence of non-matrimonial property may well be a reason to depart from equal sharing, particularly in short marriage cases, there is some debate in the judiciary about the court's approach in cases featuring non-matrimonial property.

In ***Jones v Jones***[106], Wilson LJ advocated the following approach in cases of non-matrimonial property:

(1) identify the matrimonial and non-matrimonial property;

(2) decide whether the existence of pre-matrimonial property should be reflected at all, depending on questions of duration and mingling;

(3) if it was fair to reflect the existence of non-matrimonial property, then decide how much of the non-matrimonial property should be excluded from the sharing principle;

(4) normally, divide the remaining matrimonial property equally;

106 [2011] EWCA Civ 41, [2011] 1 FLR 1723.

(5) test the fairness of the award by looking at the overall percentage division of the assets.

This approach has been applied by Mostyn J in ***FZ v SZ and another***[107], ***N v F***[108] and ***JL v SL***[109], and by Bodey J in ***S v S***[110] adopting what has become known as a formulaic approach.

Moylan J and now as Moylan LJ has advocated for a less formulaic, 'impressionist' approach to cases of non-matrimonial property, whereby the court should consider the value of all of the assets combined without precisely calculating the extent of matrimonial and non-matrimonial property, and adjust the award from 50% to reflect any non-matrimonial wealth (***Hart v Hart***[111]). In ***Hart***, Moylan LJ set out the following guidance:

> "*[85] It is, perhaps, worth reflecting that the concept of property being either matrimonial or non-matrimonial property is a legal construct. Moreover, it is a construct which is not always capable of clear identification. An asset can, of course, be entirely the former, as in many cases, or entirely the latter, as in K v L. However, it is also worth repeating that an asset can be comprise both, in the sense that it can be partly the product, or reflective, of marital endeavour and partly the product, or reflective, of a source external to the marriage...*
>
> *[86] In my view, the guidance given by Lord Nicholls in Miller remains valid today and, indeed, bears increased weight in the light of the courts' experience since that case was decided. It can, as*

---

107 [2010] EWHC 1630 (Fam).

108 *(Financial Orders: Pre-Acquired Wealth)* [2011] EWHC 586 (Fam), 2 FLR 533.

109 [2015] EWHC 360 (Fam), [2015] 2 FLR 1202.

110 [2014] EWHC 4732 (Fam),

111 [2017] EWCA Civ 1306, [2018] 2 WLR 509.

> *he said, be artificial to attempt to draw a "sharp dividing line". Valuations are a matter of opinion on which experts can differ significantly. Investigation can be "extremely expensive and of doubtful utility". The costs involved can quickly become disproportionate. Proportionality is critical both because it underpins the overriding objective and because, to quote Lord Nicholls again: "Fairness has a broad horizon".*

The main difference between the formulaic and impressionist approaches is the need to precisely quantify the matrimonial and non-matrimonial assets. Under both approaches, the court will consider the nature and source of the assets and account for non-matrimonial assets as far as is fair in the final award. In ***Versteegh v Versteegh***[112], King LJ concluded that the court may adopt either approach, depending on the degree of particularity required on the facts of the case. The impressionist approach is likely to be more appropriate where it is difficult or impossible to precisely quantify the non-matrimonial property, and the judge "*really had no option, but to give weight to the non-matrimonial assets in a more general way as part of the totality of his discretionary exercise*" (paragraph 101).

4.2.4 Mingling and matrimonialisation

Where non-matrimonial property is mingled with matrimonial property, it may lose its status as non-matrimonial property or the weight to be attached to the non-matrimonial property may be reduced. Mingling can arise where non-matrimonial property is mixed with matrimonial property or is used as the foundation upon which financial success within the marriage is based.

Non-matrimonial property is more likely to preserve its non-matrimonial nature in short marriages than long marriages as there is less time for pre-

112 [2018] EWCA Civ 1050, [2019] 2 WLR 399.

acquired assets to become mixed and mingled with the assets of the marriage.

In ***Robson v Robson***[113], which concerned a 21-year marriage, Ward LJ said:

> "*the more and the longer that wealth has been enjoyed, the less fair it is that it should be ringfenced and excluded from distribution in such a way as to render it unavailable to meet the claimant's financial needs generated by the relationship.*"

In ***K v L***[114] (another 21-year marriage), Wilson LJ said:

> "*Over time, the non-matrimonial property initially contributed has been mixed with matrimonial property in circumstances in which the contributor may be said to have accepted that it should be treated as matrimonial property or, in which, at any rate, the task of identifying its current value is too difficult*".

At paragraph 18, Wilson LJ, gave three examples of how non-matrimonial property may be mingled with matrimonial property:

> "*Thus, with respect to Baroness Hale of Richmond, I believe that the true proposition is that the importance of the source of the assets may diminish over time. Three situations come to mind:*
>
> *(a) Over time matrimonial property of such value has been acquired as to diminish the significance of the initial contribution by one spouse of non-matrimonial property.*
>
> *(b) Over time the non-matrimonial property initially contributed has been mixed with matrimonial property in circumstances in which the contributor may be said to have accepted that it should be treated as*

---

113 [2010] EWCA Civ 117, [2011] 1 FLR 751, paragraph 43.

114 [2011] EWCA Civ 550, [2012] 1 WLR 306, paragraph 21.

> *matrimonial property or in which, at any rate, the task of identifying its current value is too difficult.*
>
> *(c) The contributor of non-matrimonial property has chosen to invest it in the purchase of a matrimonial home which, although vested in his or her sole name, has – as in most cases one would expect – come over time to be treated by the parties as a central item of matrimonial property."*

In ***Standish v Standish***[115], Moylan LJ developed the examples outlined by Wilson LJ to demonstrate the circumstances in which non-matrimonial property may be said to 'matrimonialise' i.e. mingle so closely with matrimonial assets that the fundamental nature of the non-matrimonial property changes to become matrimonial. He said at paragraph 162:

> *"In my view, therefore, it would be helpful to make clear, expressly, that the concept of matrimonialisation should be applied narrowly. This is not a hard and fast line but remains a question of fairness, reflecting, as Wilson LJ said in K v L at [18], that 'the importance of the [non-marital] source of [an asset or assets] may diminish over time'. With some diffidence, I would propose the following slight reformulation of the situations to which Wilson LJ referred in K v L, having regard to the developments that have taken place since that decision as follows: (a) The percentage of the parties' assets (or of an asset), which were or which might be said to comprise or reflect the product of non-marital endeavour, is not sufficiently significant to justify an evidential investigation and/or an other than equal division of the wealth; (b) The extent to which and the manner in which non-matrimonial property has been mixed with matrimonial property mean that, in fairness, it should be included within the sharing*

[115] [2024] EWCA Civ 567, [2024] 2 FLR 966. Note that Mrs Standish secured permission to appeal to the Supreme Court and further guidance on "matrimonialisation" will follow.

> *principle; and (c) Non-marital property has been used in the purchase of the former matrimonial home, an asset which typically stands in a category of its own."*

Note that when determining whether property has been matrimonialised the court will look to the source of the asset and the parties' intentions, not the title of the property. In ***Standish***, Moylan LJ made clear that the transfer of assets into the wife's name for tax planning purposes did not change the nature of the assets, which were pre-acquired by the husband, from non-matrimonial to matrimonial. Notably in ***Standish***, the parties did not intend that the investment funds transferred to the wife should become the beneficial property of the wife, but that they should be settled on trust for the parties' children.

Determination of whether matrimonial property has become mixed and mingled is a difficult exercise to undertake precisely. In ***C v C***[116], Moylan J (as he then was) considered that after a long marriage (in that case over 20 years) it would be foolish to expect or require a party to produce a detailed account of their financial affairs at the commencement of the marriage and throughout the marriage. The same cannot be said of a short marriage, following which the court may well expect parties to recall and maintain evidence of their finances over the preceding 5 years or so.

Mingling and matrimonialisation requires time, which, in short marriage cases there will necessarily have been less of than in longer marriage cases. There may be some mingling of matrimonial and non-matrimonial property or matrimonialisation in short marriage cases. For example, in ***Miller***[117], Mr Miller's business, which he established pre-marriage, expanded and flourished as a result of his work during the marriage. However, mingling is likely to be minimal and matrimonialisation rare in short marriage cases. Even where there has been mingling or matrimonialisation, the court will ensure that non-matrimonial efforts

---

116 [2007] EWHC 2033 (Fam).

117 [2006] UKHL 24, [2006] 2 AC 618.

are reflected in the proportion of the asset which is shared, as in ***Miller***, where Mrs Miller shared less than half of the value of Mr Miller's shares to reflect his pre-matrimonial work.

4.2.5 To what extent will non-matrimonial property be shared?

Non-matrimonial property is not ignored by the courts or excluded from the court's reach. In ***Rossi v Rossi***[118], Mostyn J made the following observations of the court's approach to dividing non-matrimonial property:

> "*24.6 The non-matrimonial property is not quarantined and excluded from the court's dispositive powers. It represents an unmatched contribution by the party who brings it to the marriage. The court will decide whether it should be shared and if so in what proportions. In so deciding it will have regard to the reality that the longer the marriage, the more likely non-matrimonial property will become merged or entangled with matrimonial property. By contrast,* ***in a short marriage, non-matrimonial assets are not likely to be shared unless needs require this.***" (emphasis added)

Moylan LJ made clear in ***Standish***[119] that even where non-matrimonial property has been matrimonialised such that the property is included within the sharing principle, the starting point is not that of *equal* sharing, noting:

> "*The conclusion that it does, however, does not mean that it must be shared equally. The submission by Mr Todd that, once an asset is matrimonialised and treated as matrimonial property, it must be shared equally is unsupported by any authority and would be contrary to the objective of a fair outcome.*"

---

118 [2006] EWHC 1482 (Fam), [2007] 1 FLR 790, paragraph 24.6.

119 [2024] EWCA Civ 567, [2024] 2 FLR 966, paragraph 166.

There is significant discretion available to the court when it comes to sharing the parties' assets, particularly where it has been difficult to draw a clear line between the matrimonial and non-matrimonial property. The court will need to consider all of the s 25 factors awarding such lesser percentage than 50% that makes fair allowance for the non-matrimonial property. The court does not have to apply any particular methodology, but has a discretion as to how it arrive at a fair division[120].

Even where the court has clearly delineated the matrimonial and non-matrimonial property, it may well share all of the assets equally. The exercise depends on the length of the marriage, the nature of the non-matrimonial property and the division required for fairness in each case.

4.3 Unilateral assets

Unilateral assets are significant unmatched assets accrued by one party during a marriage as a result of their work during a short marriage, where both parties are working. Unilateral assets may be excluded from the sharing principle in the right, very rare circumstances.

The concept which became unilateral assets was described by Baroness Hale in ***Miller; McFarlane***[121]:

> "*More difficult are business or investment assets which have been generated solely or mainly by the efforts of one party. The other party has often made some contribution to the business, at least in its early days, and has continued with her agreed contribution to the welfare of the family (as did Mrs Cowan). But in these non-business-partnership, non-family asset cases, the bulk of the property has been generated by one party. Does this provide a reason for departing from the yardstick*

120 *Hart v Hart* [2017] EWCA Civ 1306, [2018] 2 WLR 509, paragraphs 94–96.

121 [2006] UKHL 24, [2006] 2 AC 618, paragraph 150.

> *of equality? On the one hand is the view, already expressed, that commercial and domestic contributions are intrinsically incommensurable. It is easy to count the money or property which one has acquired. It is impossible to count the value which the other has added to their lives together. One is counted in money or money's worth. The other is counted in domestic comfort and happiness. If the law is to avoid discrimination between the gender roles, it should regard all the assets generated in either way during the marriage as family assets to be divided equally between them unless some other good reason is shown to do otherwise.*"

The phrase 'unilateral assets' was first coined by Burton J in ***S v S***[122] to describe the main business assets where, in "*non-business-partnership, non-family asset cases, the bulk of the property has been generated by one party*", per Baroness Hale in ***Miller***[123].

In ***Charman v Charman***[124], the Court of Appeal was clear that it would be deeply discriminatory to apply the concept of unilateral assets in a long marriage (in that case 28 years). The Court therefore left open the possibility of the unilateral assets principle being applied in short marriage cases such that the unmatched earnings of one party should be excluded from the sharing principle.

---

122 *(Non-Matrimonial Property: Conduct)* [2006] EWHC 2793 (Fam).

123 [2006] UKHL 24, [2006] 2 AC 618, paragraph 150.

124 *(No.4)* [2007] EWCA Civ 503, [2007] 1 FLR 1246.

4.3.1 *Sharp v Sharp Non-Matrimonial Property: Conduct)* [2006] EWHC 2793 (Fam)

In ***Sharp v Sharp***[125], the Court of Appeal allowed an appeal by the wife from the decision of Singer J in ***JS v RS***[126], in a 'relaxation of the sharing principle' in order to recognise the wife's unilateral assets.

The facts of ***Sharp***[127] were very specific. The parties were both in their 40s and had a short marriage of 5 years with no children. The available assets were £6.9m, made up almost entirely of bonuses received by the wife during the marriage. Singer J awarded the husband £2.725m. The wife appealed, relying principally on the dictum of Baroness Hale in ***Miller*** at paragraph 153, where she stated:

> "*This is simply to recognise that in a matrimonial property regime which still starts with the premise of separate property, there is still some scope for one party to acquire and retain separate property which is not automatically to be shared equally between them. The nature and the source of the property and the way the couple have run their lives may be taken into account in deciding how it should be shared. There may be other examples. Take, for example, a genuine dual career family where each party has worked throughout the marriage and certain assets have been pooled for the benefit of the family but others have not. There may be no relationship-generated needs or other disadvantages for which compensation is warranted. We can assume that the family assets, in the sense discussed earlier, should be divided equally. But it might well be fair to leave undisturbed whatever additional surplus each has accumulated during his or her working life. However, one should be careful not to take this approach too far. What seems fair and sensible at the outset of a relationship may seem much less fair and sensible when it ends. And there could well be a sense of injustice if a*

125 [2017] EWCA Civ 408, [2018] 2 WLR 1617.

126 [2015] EWHC 2921 (Fam).

127 [2017] EWCA Civ 408, [2018] 2 WLR 1617.

dual career spouse who had worked outside as well as inside the home throughout the marriage ended up less well off than one who had only or mainly worked inside the home."

The wife argued that her case was precisely the kind of situation envisioned by Baroness Hale. Giving the lead judgment, McFarlane LJ said:

> "*[92] In the present case the wife's bonuses were not 'family assets' as categorised by Baroness Hale and, in contrast to Foster, they had not been generated by the joint efforts of the parties (Foster being a case which was held to be 'all about contribution'). It is hard to justify holding that this case is not one where 'there is still some scope for one party to acquire and retain separate property which is not automatically to be shared equally between them' (Baroness Hale para 153). By Baroness Hale's analysis at paragraph 152 the court is obliged to take account of the duration of the marriage with a view to considering reducing the husband's share to reflect the period of his domestic contribution. Further, in a case where, in contrast to the more traditional 'bread-winner' / 'home-maker' model, each partner worked full time for most of the marriage, and where there are no children, it must be necessary for the court also to evaluate the extent, if any, by which the husband's domestic contribution exceeded that of the wife.*
>
> ...
>
> *[97] The inescapable conclusion from this analysis of the speeches in Miller, in terms of the possibility of some alteration from, rather than a strict application of, the equal sharing principle in relation to short, childless marriages, where both spouses have largely been in full-time employment and where only some of their finances have been pooled, is that fairness may require a reduction from a full 50% share or the exclusion of some property from the 50% calculation. Of the five members of the Judicial Committee, only Lord Nicholls suggested a contrary view and even on his analysis the potential for some form of relaxation can be seen.*"

In ***Sharp***[128], the court was satisfied that it was necessary to depart from equal sharing in order to achieve fairness for the parties due to the combination of potentially relevant factors including their short marriage, having no children, having dual incomes and keeping their finances separate. Accordingly, the husband's award was reduced from £2.725m to £2m.

4.3.2 Post-*Sharp* cases and *E v L (Financial Remedies) [2021] EWFC 60, [2022] 1 FLR 952*

In ***XW v XH***[129], Moylan LJ considered that the concept of unilateral assets should be to be confined to cases of short, childless marriages. He was clear that the application of the concept beyond cases of short, childless marriages would be discriminatory.

In ***E v L***[130], Mostyn J considered Moylan LJ's analysis of the concept of unilateral assets applying only in short, childless marriages, and questioned why, when considering if there should be an exception to the sharing principle, it should make any difference, whether the parties had children or not?

Mostyn J made clear that there was no mention in ***Miller***[131] of the need for a marriage to be childless before the equal sharing principle could be departed from. He warned that the risk of unconscious discrimination in sharing cases is equally applicable in marriages with and without children. He stated at paragraph 28:

128 Ibid.

129 *(Financial Remedies: Business Assets)* [2019] EWCA Civ 2262, [2020] 4 WLR 22.

130 *(Financial Remedies)* [2021] EWFC 60, [2022] 1 FLR 952, paragraph 21.

131 [2006] UKHL 24, [2006] 2 AC 618.

> *"In applying the sharing principle it is not merely invidious, but extremely dangerous, for the court to attempt an evaluation of the quality of a marriage or of the arrangements made within it, as to do so will almost inevitably trigger subconscious discriminatory practices. It is for this reason that the doctrine of special contribution has to all intents and purposes been consigned to history. When the court is undertaking the application of the sharing principle, it should start and almost invariably finish with the proposition that a marriage is a marriage."*

One may consider whether the concept of 'unilateral assets' has any proper application in short marriage cases beyond ***Sharp***[132]. In ***E v L***[133] Mostyn J struggled to see why it would be necessary to consider 'unilateral assets' as a separate category of assets in short marriage cases:

> *"...There is absolutely no logical reason to draw a distinction between an accrual over a short period and an accrual over a long period. As Lord Nicholls pointed out, the statutory factor of the duration of the marriage will be reflected in the nature of things by the fact that in a short marriage the accrual will almost inevitably be less than in a longer marriage."*

Mostyn J had little choice but to acknowledge the majority view of the Court in ***Miller; McFarlane***[134], noting that there may exist a possible exception for non-family assets generated by one spouse alone during a short marriage where those assets have been kept separate and where both spouses had been financially and independently active.[135]

---

132 [2017] EWCA Civ 408, [2018] 2 WLR 1617.

133 *(Financial Remedies)* [2021] EWFC 60, [2022] 1 FLR 952, paragraph 43.

134 [2006] UKHL 24, [2006] 2 AC 618.

135 E v L, [2006] UKHL 24, [2006] 2 AC 618, paragraph 44.

Although the unilateral asset exception to the principle of equal sharing was applied in ***Sharp***[136] and acknowledged by Moylan LJ in ***XW v XH***[137], Mostyn J made clear that it will only be in rare circumstances that it would be appropriate to apply the exception, noting:

> "[45] *In Sharp, McFarlane LJ accepted at [75] that the exception would only apply in a "fringe of cases". I would go further and say that Lady Hale herself acknowledged the great rarity of the exception. Moylan LJ has made it clear that it will only be capable of being legitimately invoked in vanishingly remote circumstances. For my part I would say (as I have said before when talking about the rarity of sharing of non-matrimonial property) that a case where there can be a legitimate non-discriminatory unequal sharing of matrimonial property earned in a short marriage will be as rare as a white leopard. I have said "earned" to draw a distinction between money generated during a marriage and an asset brought into a marriage which has been "matrimonialised", such as a dwelling used as a matrimonial home. I accept that the law recognises the possibility of unequal sharing of such an asset: see Vaughan v Vaughan [2010] EWCA Civ 349 at [49] per Wilson LJ.*
>
> [46] *The reason for the rarity is obvious. The exception is founded on the notion that the value of the contributions made by one spouse during a short marriage in generating "business assets" is worth more than the value of the contributions made by the other spouse during that period. Like the now discredited doctrine of special contribution this notion gives rise to the Orwellian oxymoron that all contributions are equal but some are more equal than others. It is very difficult to escape the conclusion that discriminatory forces are underpinning this*

136 [2017] EWCA Civ 408, [2018] 2 WLR 1617.

137 *(Financial Remedies: Business Assets)* [2019] EWCA Civ 2262, [2020] 4 WLR 22.

> *notion. Hence the need to confine its application to extremely rare situations."*

Following ***E v L***[138], it will likely be difficult to argue that ***Sharp***[139] is applicable beyond its own very specific facts (short marriage, both parties working, no children, finances kept separate, major disparity in financial contribution).

4.4 Unmatched /Special Contributions

Another factor which may lead the court to depart from the principle of equal sharing of matrimonial property is a potential unmatched or 'special' contribution by one party to the welfare of the family.

Since ***White***[140] and ***Miller; McFarlane***[141], economic contributions to the marriage cannot be seen as more valuable than homemaking. In ***Miller; McFarlane,*** Baroness Hale and Lord Nicholls agreed that the notion of a special contribution should be approached in a similar way to conduct: there must be such a disparity between the parties' contributions to the welfare of the family that it would be inequitable to disregard the special contribution[142]. The kind of contribution justifying a departure from equality will not be found in the minutiae of married life. In order to impact on the equal sharing principle, a contribution needs to be exceptional, obvious and gross.

---

138 *(Financial Remedies)* [2021] EWFC 60, [2022] 1 FLR 952.

139 [2017] EWCA Civ 408, [2018] 2 WLR 1617.

140 [2000] UKHL 54, [2001] AC 596.

141 [2006] UKHL 24, [2006] 2 AC 618.

142 see paragraphs 67, 68 and 146.

In ***K v L***[143], Wilson J expounded the notion of special contributions as follows:

> "*Thus a special contribution arises in circumstances in which a spouse's contribution, direct or indirect, to the creation of matrimonial property has been so extraordinary as to dictate a departure within the sharing principle from the ordinary consequence of its equal division. It is therefore no accident that this court's reference, [in Charman] at [90], to the unlikelihood of departure from equality further than to 66.6%–33.3% was of "division of matrimonial property"*."

Unmatched contributions will usually take the form of the extremely significant earnings of one party or one party's overwhelming financial contribution to the former matrimonial home. For an analysis of unmatched contributions to the FMH, please see Chapter 6 on housing below.

4.4.1 Earnings

In ***Miller; McFarlane***[144], Lord Nicholls made clear that it will be rare for the extremely high earnings of one party during the marriage to meet the high threshold required for a special contribution. In the case of ***Miller***, the court was not satisfied that Mr Miller's high earnings represented an 'unmatched contribution'.

In ***Foster v Foster***[145], Hale LJ (as she was then) considered an appeal from a decision concerning a very short childless marriage, where both parties worked, with the wife earning substantially more than the husband. Hale LJ considered that the District Judge's approach of seeking to put the

143 *(Non-Matrimonial Property: Special Contribution)* [2011] EWCA Civ 550, [2012] 1 WLR 306, paragraph 21.

144 [2006] UKHL 24, [2006] 2 AC 618, paragraph 68.

145 [2003] EWCA Civ 565, [2003] 2 FLR 299.

parties back into the position they had been before the marriage, by giving the parties back what they brought into the marriage and dividing the surplus equally between them, was a faultless approach. The court rejected the wife's contention that her remarkable earnings during the marriage should be seen as an unmatched contribution and concluded that there was no reason to depart from equal sharing. Hale LJ said at paragraphs 18-19:

> "*There can be no justification for treating differences in income any differently from differences between breadwinning and homemaking. These days things are rarely as simple as one breadwinner and one homemaker. Both may work equally hard but in jobs which are unequally remunerated. They may agree that one should work part-time, or take a career break, in order to enable the other to move or take promotion. They may agree that one should work full-time at the outset to enable the other to gain qualifications which will then enable the first to concentrate on domestic responsibilities. As it happens, differences in income and career progression are also frequently the result of inequalities in earning power between the sexes, although not always, as this case shows. If both go out to work and pool their incomes or spend a comparable proportion of their incomes for the benefit of the family, it would be a surprising proposition indeed if they were not to be regarded as having made an equal contribution to the family home or other family assets…*
>
> *[19] The duration of the marriage will obviously be relevant in cases where one party's earning capacity may have been seriously affected by a long period devoted to homemaking and childrearing, but Miss Boyd eventually had to accept that where a substantial surplus had been generated by their joint efforts, it could not matter whether they had taken a short or a long time to do so.*"

The case law makes clear that special contributions in the form of one party's earnings will be exceptional. In ***Lambert v Lambert***[146] Bodey J said that the characteristics required of a special contribution:

> "*have to be of a wholly exceptional nature, such that it would very obviously be inconsistent with the objective of achieving fairness (ie it would create an unfair outcome) for them to be ignored.*"

Since ***Miller; McFarlane***[147], cases of special contribution have been reserved for cases of very significant wealth. In ***SK v TK***[148], Moor J rejected the husband's submission that he had made a special contribution where the parties' total assets were £18m, as the husband's business success had "*not been so great as to generate truly vast wealth*".

Examples of cases where the court has accepted a special contribution argument are ***Charman v Charman***[149], ***Cooper-Hohn v Cooper-Hohn***[150] and ***XW v XH***[151] where the total assets were £131, US $1.5bn and £520m respectively.

In ***Work v Gray***[152], the Court of Appeal summarised the following guidance to be applied when considering whether a contribution amounts to a special contribution:

> *(1) the characteristics or circumstances which would result in a departure from equality have to be of a wholly exceptional nature such*

[146] [2002] EWCA Civ 1685,

[147] [2006] UKHL 24, [2006] 2 AC 618.

[148] [2013] EWHC 834 (Fam)

[149] *(No 4)* [2007] EWCA Civ 503 [2007] 1 FLR 1246, see paragraph 90.

[150] [2014] EWHC 4122 (Fam), [2015] 1 FLR 745, see paragraph 282.

[151] [2017] EWFC 76, [2019] 1 FLR 581.

[152] [2017] EWCA Civ 270, [2017] 3 WLR 535.

> *that it would very obviously be inconsistent with the objective of achieving fairness for them to be ignored;*
>
> *(2) exceptional earnings are to be regarded as a factor pointing away from equality of division when, but only when, it would be inequitable to proceed otherwise;*
>
> *(3) only if there is such disparity in the respective contributions to the welfare of the family that it will be inequitable to disregard it should this be taken into account in determining their shares;*
>
> *(4) it is extremely important to avoid discrimination against the homemaker;*
>
> *(5) the amount of wealth alone may be so extraordinary as to make it easy for the party who generated it to claim an exceptional and individual quality which deserves special treatment; often however he or she will need independently to establish such a quality; this requires the court to look both at the nature of the contribution and to determine whether it derives from an exceptional and individual quality; and*
>
> *(6) there is no identified threshold for such a claim to succeed.*"

In short marriage cases, there will necessarily have been less time for one party to accrue the significant earnings to reach the high threshold required for a special contribution. A spouse who has earned significantly during a short marriage is more likely to succeed in arguing that the unilateral assets exception applies than the special contribution exception, although that exception is itself rare.

4.5 Children

The courts have consistently made clear that the presence of children makes no difference to a sharing claim, no matter how short or long the marriage is. Children are only relevant to needs. In ***E v L***[153], on the distinction between a childless marriage and a marriage with children, Mostyn J concluded:

> "*[29] In my judgment for the court to start asking why there are no children, and whether this denotes a lesser extent of commitment to the relationship, is to make windows into people's souls, and should be avoided at all costs.*
>
> *[30] It is not clear to me from where this factor of childlessness derives. An analysis of Miller v Miller; McFarlane v McFarlane [2006] 1 FLR 1186 shows that childlessness is not part of the reasoning of Baroness Hale of Richmond and Lord Mance. It is true that the Miller marriage was childless. At para [41] Lord Nicholls of Birkenhead referred to the absence of children, but recorded that the couple had been trying for one and that Mrs Miller had suffered a miscarriage. No one suggested that this sad failure denoted "a completely different category of commitment".*
>
> *[31] Childlessness was not a reason that the House of Lords upheld the unequal division of the acquest in that case.*
>
> …
>
> *[34] In my judgment this factor should be banished from any consideration of whether there should be a departure from the application of the equal sharing principle. Whatever may be the true construction of that section of Baroness Hale of Richmond's speech, it does not include bringing into consideration the childlessness of the marriage, if that were the case.*"

153 *(Financial Remedies)* [2021] EWFC 60, [2022] 1 FLR 952.

It was confirmed that Mostyn J's reasoning in ***E v L*** certainly applies to short marriage cases by Peel J in ***VV v VV***[154] where he stated:

> "*I agree with Mostyn J at para [28] of E v L that it is dangerous for the court to evaluate the quality of a marriage …*"

[154] [2022] EWFC 41, [2023] 1 FLR 170 at paragraph 44.

CHAPTER FIVE

COMPENSATION IN A SHORT MARRIAGE CASE

5.1 What is the compensation principle?

The concept of compensation for relationship-generated economic disadvantage first emerged in ***Miller v Miller; McFarlane v McFarlane***[155]. Mrs McFarlane received an enhanced award for periodical payments to reflect an element of compensation. Mrs McFarlane had given up her career as a solicitor in the City in order to focus on raising the parties' children, allowing Mr McFarlane to pursue his lucrative career as an accountant. As a result of the choices made by the parties during the marriage, there was a significant economic disparity between the parties' earning capacities at the end of their marriage compared to the relatively equal positions they had been in at the beginning of the marriage. Mrs McFarlane's enhanced periodical payment award was intended to balance the economic disparity between the parties in terms of their earning capacity.

Explaining the rationale for the compensation principle in ***Miller; McFarlane***, Baroness Hale said:

> *"[138] … But another source of need is having had to look after children or other family members in the past. Many parents have seriously compromised their ability to attain self-sufficiency as a result of past family responsibilities. Even if they do their best to re-enter the employment market, it will often be at a lesser level than before, and they were hardly ever be able to make up what they have lost in pension entitlements. A further source of need may be the way in which the*

[155] [2006] UKHL 24, [2006] 2 AC 618.

parties chose to run their life together. Even dual career families are difficult to manage with completely equal opportunity for both. Compromises often have to be made by one so that the other can get ahead. All couples throughout their lives together have to make choices about who will do what, sometimes forced upon them by circumstances such as redundancy or low pay, sometimes freely made in the interests of them both. The needs generated by such choices are a perfectly sound rationale for adjusting the parties' respective resources in compensation.

...

[140] A second rationale, which is closely related to need, is compensation for relationship-generated disadvantage. Indeed, some consider that provision for need is compensation for relationship-generated disadvantage. But the economic disadvantage generated by the relationship may go beyond need, however generously interpreted. The best example is a wife, like Mrs McFarlane, who has given up what would very probably have been a lucrative and successful career. If the other party, who has been the beneficiary of the choices made during the marriage, is a high earner with a substantial surplus over what is required to meet both parties' needs, then a premium above needs can reflect that relationship-generated disadvantage."

For the compensation principle to be engaged, there needs to be an element of sacrifice by the financially-weaker party of their own earning capacity, with their sacrifice enabling the financially stronger party to increase their own earning capacity.

This chapter will consider:

- How the court approaches the compensation principle
- Warnings against pursuing a compensation claim
- Examples of compensation based awards

5.2 How does the court approach the compensation principle?

Like sharing, compensation is only relevant as a concept where the parties' needs are comfortably met and there is a surplus of assets to be divided between the parties. Any compensation award should be paid in addition to a sharing award.

The compensation principle does not require a direct causal link between the marriage and the economic disadvantage suffered. The compensation principle should be distinguished from the needs principle in this respect, as needs must usually be relationship generated[156]. Compensation may be payable even where the economically-disadvantaged party is able to earn some income of their own on marital breakdown[157].

A compensation award may be reflected in periodical payments[158], a lump sum[159] or a deferred lump sum[160].

In ***Miller; McFarlane***[161], Lords Nicholls and Mance and Baroness Hale were clear that the principles of need, sharing and compensation apply equally in cases of short marriages as long marriages.

However, it should be noted that compensation is unlikely to play a significant part in short marriage cases, principally because there will have been less time during short marriages for any significant disadvantage to be generated by one party, compared to during longer

---

156 ND v GD *(Financial Remedies)* [2022] EWFC 53, paragraph 52.

157 Per Baroness Hale in Miller v Miller; McFarlane v McFarlane [2006] UKHL 24, [2006] 2 AC 618.

158 Miller v Miller; McFarlane v McFarlane [2006] UKHL 24, [2006] 2 AC 618.

159 *RC v JC* [2020] EWHC 466 (Fam).

160 *H v H* [2014] EWHC 760 (Fam), [2014] 2 FLR, 1338.

161 [2006] UKHL 24, [2006] 2 AC 618.

marriages. The McFarlane marriage was a medium-long marriage of 18 years. By the time of the hearing in House of Lords Mrs McFarlane had been out of work for 15 years, and would have faced considerable difficulty returning to work even at the level she was at pre-marriage, as a result of her long career-break. This situation simply cannot arise in short marriage cases. Even where a party has taken time off work to care for children, after a short marriage, they can only have been out of work for a maximum of 5 years, and would be very unlikely to face insurmountable difficulties in returning to work. The extent that one party would be disadvantaged in terms of returning to work could most likely be met by way of a needs award, without the need to engage with the compensation principle.

There is some overlap between the concepts of compensation, needs and sharing. Where one party decides to give up their career in order to focus on domestic life, they will be recognised as having made an equal contribution to the family as compared with the party who worked, and this will be reflected in equal sharing of the fruits of the marriage[162]. Similarly, a party's impaired earning capacity as a result of not working during the marriage may be reflected in their needs award. Lord Nicholls was clear in ***Miller; McFarlane***[163] that the three concepts are all distinct, but nevertheless caution should be taken to ensure that a compensation award does not result in 'double-counting' for the compensated party. The overlap between compensation, needs and sharing perhaps explains why there are so few examples in the case law of successful compensation claims.

In ***SA v PA***[164] Mostyn J rejected the wife's application for a compensatory element within her award. He considered ***Miller; McFarlane*** and the

---

162 e.g. see *Hvorostovsky v Hvorostovsky* [2009] EWCA Civ 791, [2009] 2 FLR 1574.

163 [2006] UKHL 24, [2006] 2 AC 618.

164 *(Pre-Marital Agreement: Compensation)* [2014] EWHC 392 (Fam), [2014] 2 FLR 1028.

subsequent authorities and drew together the following principles on the compensation principle at paragraph 36:

> "(i) *It will only be in a very rare and exceptional case where the principle will be capable of being successfully invoked.*
>
> *(ii) Such a case will be one where the court can say without any speculation, ie with almost near certainty, that the claimant gave up a very high earning career which had it not been foregone would have led to earnings at least equivalent to that presently enjoyed by the respondent.*
>
> *(iii) Such a high earning career will have been practised by the claimant over an appreciable period during the marriage. Proof of this track-record is key.*
>
> *(iv) Once these findings have been made compensation will be reflected by fixing the periodical payments award (or the multiplicand if this aspect is being capitalised by Duxbury) towards the top end of the discretionary bracket applicable for a needs assessment on the facts of the case. Compensation ought not be reflected by a premium or additional element on top of the needs based award.*"

In ***Waggott v Waggott***[165], the Court of Appeal expressly discouraged extensive, expensive exploration of the issue of compensation. However, the Court noted at paragraph 139 that if a compensation claim is pursued as a necessary factual foundation:

> "*the court would have to determine, on a balance of probabilities, that the applicant's career would have resulted in them having resources greater than those which they will be awarded by application of either the need principle or the sharing principle. Further, the court must*

165 [2018] EWCA Civ 727, [2018] 2 FLR 406.

separately determine whether, and if so how, this factor should be reflected in the award so as to ensure that it is fair to both parties"

5.3 Warnings against pursuing a compensation claim

The case law reflects a tendency to discourage litigants from pursuing claims for compensation, particularly where there is insufficient capital to meet a party's future maintenance needs.

In ***VB v JP***[166] Mark Potter P was clear that compensation should not be isolated as an aim, but subsumed within the needs and sharing principles where possible. He said:

> "*… Attempts under the rubric of compensation to isolate and quantify the level of income or earning capacity sacrificed by a wife years after the event for the purpose of calculating a premium element on the award, constitutes a search for precision which is to be discouraged both on the grounds of policy and practicality, and which goes beyond what is required or generally appropriate in the exercise required of the court under s 25.*" (paragraph 52)

> "*any compensatory element is best dealt with by a generous assessment of her continuing needs unrestricted by purely budgetary considerations, in the light of the contribution of the wife to the marriage and the broad effect of the sacrifice of her own earning capacity upon her ability to provide for her needs.*" (paragraph 59)

In short marriage cases, the needs principles is particularly likely to take precedence over the compensation principle. Even where the court is satisfied that one party's earning capacity is impaired as a result of the marriage, the deficit generated by that disadvantage is likely to be subsumed within an analysis of their needs, generously interpreted.

166 [2008] EWHC 112 (Fam), [2008] 1 FLR 742.

An example of the court's focusing on needs over compensation is the pre-***White*** case of ***C v C***[167], which concerned marriage of just 9.5 months, where the Court was satisfied that the wife was unable to work as a result of her health issues. In that case, the wife's needs were generously interpreted and met by means of a joint lives order for periodical payments. The court noted that ***C v C*** was highly unusual in terms of its facts.

Another example of generous-needs interpretation in lieu of compensation in a short marriage case is ***G v G***[168]. In ***G v G***, Charles J awarded the wife a £1.5m lump sum in addition to periodical payments for 9 years in circumstances where she had given up her career as a barrister to care for the parties' child, and could not be expected to work full-time for some time.

The court has made clear that the threshold for a successful compensation claim is high. In ***McCartney v Mills-McCartney***[169], Heather Mills argued she was entitled to compensation because her marriage to Paul McCartney had damaged her career as a model and public speaker. The court was clear the compensation principle was not engaged and that Heather Mills had exaggerated her case that she had been wealthy before the relationship with the husband. There was certainly no evidence that Paul McCartney had restricted his wife's career and charitable activities. In that case, Heather Mills's award was entirely based on her needs, very generously interpreted.

In ***RC v JC***[170], in which Moor J was satisfied that that the wife had suffered relationship-generated disadvantage justifying an award for

167 *(Financial relief: Short Marriage)* [1997] 2 FLR 26.

168 *(Financial Remedies: Short Marriage: Trust Assets)* [2012] EWHC 167 (Fam), [2012] 2 FLR 48.

169 [2008] EWHC 401 (Fam), [2008] 1 FLR 1508.

170 [2020] EWHC 466 (Fam), paragraph 72.

compensation, he warned litigants against pursuing a compensation claim, stating:

> "*litigants should think long and hard before launching a claim for relationship-generated disadvantage and they should not take this judgment as any sort of "green light" to do so unless the circumstances are truly exceptional.*"

5.4 Examples of compensation awards

In ***H v H***[171], a wife who had been a qualified accountant before leaving her career to look after the parties' children was entitled to a compensation element of £400,000 to be paid as a lump sum by the husband upon his retirement. Note that ***H v H*** was a variation of periodical payments application by the husband after a 20-year marriage. Coleridge J said on the proper applicability and need for the compensation principle at paragraph 66:

> "*I should only finally say that I agree with recent pronouncements about the dangers inherent in attributing special weight to arguments about compensation. However, there remain a very small number of cases where it stares the court in the face and to ignore it and simply approach the case on the basis of the more simplistic 'needs' arguments does not do full justice to a wife who has sacrificed the added security of generating her own substantial earning capacity, as this wife undoubtedly did. I doubt in the end she is any worse off financially because her investment in the family enabled the husband to generate these enormous returns which she has fully participated in. However, the building up of a secure earning capacity over a working life is a greater security to an individual spouse, whether husband or wife, than merely being dependent on the future income-generating resources of one's former partner however successful.*"

171 [2014] EWHC 760 (Fam), [2014] 2 FLR 1338.

Lauder v Lauder[172] was another variation of maintenance application, this time by the wife. The court was satisfied on appeal that the wife's modest earning capacity was a direct result of the parties' decision during the marriage that the wife should be a stay at home mother. She was at a severe disadvantage in the labour market following a long marriage of 20 years, at 70 years old, and she was to be compensated accordingly, in addition to a generous interpretation of needs.

In ***RC v JC***[173], which concerned a marriage of around 10 years, the court was satisfied that the wife had suffered relationship-generated disadvantage as she had given up her career as a solicitor in the same firm as her husband in order to look after the parties' children, with the husband being fully supportive of her decision. Moor J considered that the wife's economic disadvantage justified a lump-sum award for compensation of £400,000 in addition to her sharing-entitlement and generous maintenance award. The £400,000 represented £100,000 per year for each year that the husband would continue to work.

In ***TM v KM***[174], His Honour Judge Hess was satisfied that the wife was entitled to an element of compensation where both parties had had successful careers in finance when they commenced their relationship, and the wife had sacrificed her career in order to move to England and the Middle East with the husband and care for the parties' children. Note the marriage was 17 years in duration.

In ***AT v BT***[175], the wife had been an extremely successful accountant at a top Private Equity house when the parties met: she was the youngest ever partner and highest paid woman in the company. The wife had to give up her position as the partners in the company where she worked

[172] [2007] EWHC 1227 (Fam), [2007] 2 FLR 802.

[173] [2020] EWHC 466 (Fam).

[174] [2022] EWFC 155.

[175] [2023] EWHC 3531 (Fam).

were concerned that the wife was engaged to the husband, who was a senior executive at a rival private equity business. Francis J was clear that to ignore the compensation principle in that case would "*be an affront to the proper application of the compensation principle*". Francis J accounted for the compensation element of the wife's award by including all assets in the asset schedule, including alleged non-matrimonial assets, and sharing them equally. Again, the marriage was of medium-long duration.

It is worth noting that there are no reported decisions where the compensation-based award has been made in a short-marriage case. As already stated, in short marriage cases, any compensation element is likely to be subsumed within a needs award, as in ***C v C***[176] and ***G v G***[177].

176 *(Financial relief: Short Marriage)* [1997] 2 FLR 26.

177 *(Financial Remedies: Short Marriage: Trust Assets)* [2012] EWHC 167 (Fam), [2012] 2 FLR 48.

CHAPTER SIX

HOUSING IN A SHORT MARRIAGE CASE

6.1 How may the court provide for housing?

Both parties to a marriage have a need to be housed following the conclusion of the marriage. Housing provision will usually be the first needs based consideration of the court when it comes to assess the parties' needs and divide their assets.

The court may make provision for housing by way of:

- A lump sum order (MCA 1973, s 23(10(c))

- A property adjustment order - one party's share of a property is transferred to the other or to another (MCA 1973, s 24)

- *Mesher* order - a property is held by the parties for each other on trust in specific shares, with the sale deferred until a trigger event (MCA 1973 s 24(1)(b)).

- Order for the sale of a property with directions for how the proceeds of sale should be divided (MCA 1973, s 24A)

- Transfer of tenancy order (Family Law Act 1997, Schedule 7).

Where there is a child (or children) of the family, the welfare of the child is the first consideration of the court. Housing provision for the children must be considered. Where there are insufficient assets available to meet the needs of both parties, the court will prioritise the need to provide stable and secure housing for any children of the family. Therefore, when assessing needs, the presence of children will usually be given more weight than the fact that the marriage was short.

6.2 Reversion-type arguments

In several short marriage cases, it has been argued by the husband that housing provision should not be provided for the wife outright, but settled for the benefit of the child, with a reversion to the husband at a later date. In cases where the husband has significant assets to purchase a property for the wife outright, these arguments have consistently been rejected by the courts.

In ***C v C***[178], following a marriage of just nine and a half months the wife was awarded a lump sum of £195,000 to purchase a property for herself and the parties' child. The husband appealed and argued that the judge at first instance was wrong to provide the wife with outright housing provision. In his view, a property should be settled on the child during his minority, with reversion to the husband when the child was grown up (akin to a schedule 1-type order). The Court of Appeal rejected the husband's submissions and noted that the reasoning of the first instance judge could not be plainly wrong.

A similar argument was advanced by the husband in ***B v B***[179], a case in which the marriage lasted less than one year. The husband's argument that any property purchased for the benefit of the wife and the child should be held on the terms of a *Mesher* order was rejected at first instance and on appeal and the husband was ordered to pay the wife a lump sum of £175,000 to enable her to purchase a house. A *Mesher* order would fail to recognise the substantial contribution that the wife would make in the years to come by caring for the parties' child. Further, the wife, unlike the husband, would have little prospect of generating capital

---

178 *(financial relief: short marriage)* [1997] 2 FLR 26.

179 *(Mesher Order)*[2002] EWHC 3106 (Fam), [2003] 2 FLR 285.

during the life-time of a *Mesher* order to enable her to purchase her own property. In explaining why a Mesher was inappropriate, Munby J said:

> *"At the end of the day, it seems to me that there are two factors in particular which point strongly to the conclusion that there should not be a Mesher order. The first is that the wife's realistic prospects of being able to generate capital of her own between now and the date when one of the Mesher triggers would operate is small, whereas there is every reason to believe with a significant degree of confidence that well before (and it may very well be long before) a Mesher trigger operates, this husband will be able to generate a substantial degree of capital for himself over and above that capital which, in any event, remains with him notwithstanding the deputy district judge's order.*
>
> *That inequality of outcome, as it seems to me it will be if a Mesher order is made, is an outcome brought about by the fact that this wife will have to devote the best part of those years of her working life which would otherwise enable her to generate capital and earn at a higher rate in later life, to the job of bringing up W. That is, albeit in the future, a major, a very substantial, contribution which she brings to this marriage. That is a contribution which, as it seems to me, will not fairly be recognised and reflected in the award which is made if that award is subject to a Mesher charge.*
>
> *The other point, as I have already mentioned, is that as it seems to me, the advantage in financial terms which will accrue to this husband were there to be a Mesher charge, would confer on him a benefit which, in comparison with his other likely resources, is comparatively modest. Whereas, on the other hand, the financial burden that will be suffered by the wife if there is a Mesher order requiring her to sell the house in which she and W have lived at one of the suggested trigger points, will throw upon her a financial burden much more significant in terms of her economy than the corresponding financial advantage will have upon the husband's domestic economy.*

> *That, again, as it seems to me, would produce an outcome that is unfair rather than fair. It would be an outcome that does not reflect the contribution which she has made and will continue to make.*"

In ***X v D***[180], a case in which the parties were married for just four months but had one child together, the court rejected the husband's submission that his company could purchase a property to be used by the wife until their child was 21. The husband had substantial assets of some £8m, the husband's earning capacity was far in excess of the wife's, and given that the wife was in her fifties, she had little ability to build up capital of her own. The court ordered the husband to pay the wife £525,000 to enable her to purchase a property mortgage-free.

In ***UD v TQ***[181], following a 2-year marriage, the husband sought for the property that the wife lived in with the parties' child to be sold when the child turned 18 and the proceeds divided equally. HHJ Hess rejected the husband's submission and ordered him to transfer his interest in the property to the wife. In addition, the husband was ordered to transfer W £100,000 to pay off her debts and redeem her mortgage. HHJ Hess said at paragraph 27:

> "*The parties were married and it would not in my view be appropriate to make a Children Act 1989 Schedule 1 type order which returned any property to the husband when BD has grown up – her housing needs extend beyond BD's minority.*"

6.3 Stockpiling

In cases where the parties are relatively wealthy, arguments have been successfully made following short marriages that the primary carer of a child should be entitled to an element of stock-piling or savings.

---

180 [2023] EWFC 332 (B).

181 [2024] EWFC 119 (B).

In ***Fields v Fields***[182], the parties were married for 8.5 years, had two children and capital of around £6m (£4m liquid). Holman J accepted that the wife needed a flat on the ground floor or with a lift due to an issue with her knee, and that she needed to live in a central London location, as that is how the parties lived during the marriage. She was awarded £2.55m for housing. Holman J accepted the wife's argument that she was entitled to 'stockpile' funds for a pension or savings for herself in the same way the husband was going to contribute to his pension, given her age of 42. The husband was ordered to pay the wife a stockpiling provision of £100,000 per annum, which the wife could use to pay a capital mortgage on a home which exceeded her needs, so that she could downsize and access the capital available in her home when she needed it.

Similarly, in ***AB v FC (Short Marriage: Needs: Stockpiling)***[183], Roberts J accepted that the wife was entitled to 'stockpiling' provision of £80,000 per annum following her 19 month marriage to a professional footballer that produced one child. The parties had lived in luxurious rented accommodation during the marriage and had no assets other than a house in Miami in the husband's name worth just under $1m. The wife sought a budget to enable her to purchase a property for her and the child of the family worth £1.1m (comparable to the former matrimonial home. Roberts J said at paragraph 77:

> "*It has to be borne carefully in mind that there is an inter-relationship between the level at which future needs will be assessed and the period during which a court is likely to find those needs should be met by the paying former spouse. The longer the period, the more likely it is that the court will decline to assess those needs on the basis of a standard of living which replicates that enjoyed during the marriage. In my judgment those principles apply in this case equally to the assessment of W's housing and income needs. Whilst I understand that the rented*

182 [2015] EWHC 1670 (Fam), [2016] 1 FLR 1186.

183 [2016] EWHC 3285 (Fam), [2017] 4 WLR 35.

property in the north of England which was the former matrimonial home was a very comfortable and spacious property with all the trappings of 'life lived in the fast lane', it was not a property in which either of these parties had any financial interest whatsoever. It was their home for a very short period of time and thus its use as a benchmark for W's future housing needs is, in my judgment, of limited significance regardless of the type of property which H is renting on a short term basis close to his team's headquarters in Europe."

Roberts J concluded that the wife's needs were for purchased accommodation as opposed to rented, but that the standard of property she needed was lower than the former matrimonial home. The husband was ordered to sell the Miami property and pay 36% of the proceeds or £270,000 from the proceeds (whichever is greater) to the wife, in order to enable her to purchase a property worth £700,000 with a mortgage. The £80,000 per annum stockpiling fund would enable the wife to repay the mortgage.

Key to both of these cases was the husband's income. The husband in ***Fields*** earned c.£1.37m per annum and the husband in ***AB v FC*** earned c.£1m per annum. The court sought to ensure that the wives would be able to meet their needs and the needs of their children at a point in the future when the husbands were no longer able to provide for them at the current scale.

6.4 Contributions and pre-acquired wealth

Pre-acquired wealth and significant contributions to the family home have more relevance in short marriage cases than long marriage cases. See section 4.2 on non-matrimonial property, above, for more details.

There is some dispute in the authorities as to whether the parties' family home can be non-matrimonial property. In ***Miller; McFarlane***[184], Lord

[184] [2006] UKHL 24, [2006] 2 AC 618, paragraph 22.

Nicholls considered whether the family home would always be a matrimonial asset, regardless of the length of the marriage and therefore always rife for sharing:

> "*... The parties' matrimonial home, even if this was brought into the marriage at the outset by one of the parties, usually has a central place in any marriage. So it should normally be treated as matrimonial property for this purpose. As already noted, in principle the entitlement of each party to a share of the matrimonial property is the same however long or short the marriage may have been.*"

In ***S v S***[185], Burton J stated the family home would be matrimonial property whatever the source of the property or duration of the marriage. In ***K v L***[186], Wilson LJ recognised the importance of the family home in any marriage but used the example of non-matrimonial contributions towards a family home to demonstrate that the source of the assets may diminish over time. Wilson LJ therefore left open the option of a family home or part of it being non-matrimonial.

The Court of Appeal made clear in ***Standish v Standish***[187] that the family home is "*an asset which typically stands in a category of its own*". The family home will always have a significant place in a marriage, so it is difficult to argue that the family home is non-matrimonial. However, recent case law makes clear that the courts may be willing to consider that one party's unmatched contribution to the family home justifies a departure from the equal sharing of the family home.

---

185 *(Non-Matrimonial Property: Conduct)* [2006] EWHC 2793 (Fam), [2007] 1 FLR 1496.

186 *(Non-Matrimonial Property: Special Contribution)* [2011] EWCA Civ 550, [2011] 2 FLR 980.

187 [2024] EWCA Civ 567, [2024] 2 FLR 966, paragraph 163.

In ***JL v SL***[188], Mostyn J stated that the family home does not necessarily need to be divided equally:

> "*But even the matrimonial home is not necessarily divided equally under the sharing principle; an unequal division may be justified if unequal contributions to its acquisition can be demonstrated.*"

In ***S v AG***[189], Mostyn J considered a matrimonial home which had been purchased and renovated entirely with lottery winnings received by the wife four years before the end of the marriage. Mostyn J noted that the wife's funds had been 'matirmonialised' as they had been put in the family home, but considered that the non-matrimonial source of the lottery winnings and the wife's unmatched contribution should be reflected in the overall award. Mostyn J stated:

> "*even if there has been much mingling, the original non-matrimonial source of the money often demands reflection in the award*"[190]

Although ***S v AG*** concerned a 27-year marriage, the case may well be applicable in short marriage cases because the non-matrimonial lottery winnings were received only 4 years prior to the parties' separation and the family home purchased and renovated thereafter. Mostyn J specifically relied on the fact that the husband had not lived in the family home for long in reaching his conclusion that he should only be entitled to 15-20% of the equity in the family home. The same logic will apply in short marriage cases where the parties are living in a property purchased (almost) entirely by one party, and have not lived in the property for long.

---

188 *(No 2) (Appeal: Non-Matrimonial Property)* [2015] EWHC 360 (Fam), [2015] 2 FLR 1202, paragraph 27.

189 *(Financial Orders: Lottery Prize)* [2011] EWHC 2637 (Fam), [2012] 1 FLR 651.

190 Ibid. paragraph 8.

In ***D v D***[191] the court determined that it would not be fair to subject the entirety of the family home to equal sharing in circumstances where the entire purchase and full renovation of it were funded by the husband's father just 3 years before the 8-year marriage ended, and the property was registered in the husband's sole name. The property was not entirely non-matrimonial in the circumstances of the parties' 8 year marriage (explicitly described as 'not short'), their having two children, and the husband's own proposal for the wife and children to remain in the family home for a further 17 years. Cohen J concluded that 40% of the home would be deemed to be a matrimonial asset and he would add to the acquest £1.648m to represent that figure.

In ***Vaughan v Vaughan***[192], Wilson LJ considered a former matrimonial home that had been purchased by the husband with inheritance monies and owned mortgage-free prior to the marriage. Even though the parties had had a long marriage and the family home had been placed in the parties' joint names towards the end of the marriage, Wilson LJ decided that the District and Circuit Judges had placed insufficient weight on the husband's prior ownership of the home and allowed his appeal.

In ***FB v PS***[193], Moor J determined that a former matrimonial home which the parties lived in for 15 years, with an equity of £3,500,000 should be removed from the asset schedule less £500,000 to be shared between the parties. The husband's father effectively owned the property before the marriage, paid for refurbishment works to the property and transferred the property to the husband's sole name during the marriage. Moor J was satisfied that the husband's contribution was unmatched and needed to be reflected in the award. He said at paragraph 120:

---

191 *(Financial Remedies: Pre-Marital Agreement and Unequal Shares)* [2020] EWHC 857 (Fam), [2020] 2 FLR 662.

192 [2007] EWCA Civ 1085, [2008] 1 FLR 1108.

193 [2015] EWHC 2797 (Fam), [2016] 2 FLR 697.

> *"AR was therefore the matrimonial home for some 15 years. Given the dicta of Lord Nicholls of Birkenhead, I can only find that it is matrimonial property but I do not accept that this means that it is to be shared between the parties. AR was not acquired by the parties themselves during the marriage. It had been a matrimonial home of TS and his wife, since 1982. The husband and his siblings were brought up there. The transfer itself is a very significant unmatched contribution, now worth some £3.5m gross."*

Unmatched contributions to the former matrimonial home will be particularly relevant in cases of short marriages for the same reasons that non-matrimonial property is more relevant in short marriage cases: there has been less time for mingling and matrimonialisation. However, note with the family home there will always have been some element of matrimonialisation by virtue of the parties' living in the property. A proportion of the family home will be shared, the question will be how much.

CHAPTER SEVEN

INCOME NEEDS / SPOUSAL MAINTENANCE IN A SHORT MARRIAGE CASE

7.1 What is a spousal maintenance order?

Spousal maintenance is an 'income' order that the court can order (along with orders for capital and pensions) pursuant to the Matrimonial Causes Act (MCA) 1973 and Civil Partnership Act (CPA) 2004. The spousal maintenance order will required one party to pay the other party a fixed amount at fixed intervals (usually monthly) for a specified period.

References to 'maintenance' in this section refer only to spousal maintenance and not to child maintenance, which is a separate matter.

The court's power to order periodical payments following a final divorce order is derived from MCA 1973 s 23(1)(a). The court also has the power to make secured periodical payments orders under MCA 1973 s 23(1)(b). The power to make an order for maintenance before a final divorce order is derived from MCA 1973 s 22, which deals with maintenance pending suit, and s 22ZA and s 22ZB, which deal with legal services payment orders.

7.2 How does the court approach the issue of maintenance?

Where one party seeks a maintenance order, the court will consider, first, whether a maintenance order should be made at all, secondly, the amount of maintenance that should be ordered, and thirdly, the duration for which any maintenance should be paid. Central to these questions is the needs of the financially-weaker party and the income and earning capacity of both parties. There is no formula which the court will apply when considering maintenance, there is a broad discretion available to the court when considering whether to order maintenance, with the court's task to achieve fairness in the circumstances.

On considering questions of maintenance, the court has a duty to endeavour to achieve a clean break between the parties where possible[194]. This means the court must consider whether it is necessary to make a maintenance order, whether maintenance could be met by way of capitalised maintenance, and the duration of any maintenance order, noting that maintenance should only be ordered for so long as is necessary for the financially-weaker party to adjust to independence without undue hardship.

Maintenance orders may be made by way of capitalisation or for the short, medium or long-term, i.e:

- Capitalisation: clean break, with maintenance to be paid as a lump sum with reference to Duxbury/Ogden tables.

- Short-term: e.g. for a few years while there is adjustment to independence.

- Medium-term: e.g. while children are young/in education.

- Long-term: e.g. until retirement or for the parties' joint-lives.

In *SS v NS (Spousal Maintenance)*[195] where Mostyn J summarised the principles to be applied by the court when considering an application for spousal maintenance:

[194] Matrimonial Causes Act 1973, s 25A

[195] [2014] EWHC 4183, [2015] 2 FLR 1124, at [46]

"Pulling the threads together it seems to me that the relevant principles in play on an application for spousal maintenance are as follows:

(i) A spousal maintenance award is properly made where the evidence shows that choices made during the marriage have generated hard future needs on the part of the claimant. ***Here the duration of the marriage and the presence of children are pivotal factors****.*

(ii) An award should only be made by reference to needs, save in a most exceptional case where it can be said that the sharing or compensation principle applies.

(iii) Where the needs in question are not causally connected to the marriage the award should generally be aimed at alleviating significant hardship.

(iv) In every case the court must consider a termination of spousal maintenance with a transition to independence as soon as it is just and reasonable. A term should be considered unless the payee would be unable to adjust without undue hardship to the ending of payments. A degree of (not undue) hardship in making the transition to independence is acceptable.

(v) If the choice between an extendable term and a joint lives order is finely balanced the statutory steer should militate in favour of the former.

(vi) The marital standard of living is relevant to the quantum of spousal maintenance but is not decisive. That standard should be carefully weighed against the desired objective of eventual independence.

(vii) The essential task of the judge is not merely to examine the individual items in the claimant's income budget but also to stand back and to look at the global total and to ask if it represents a fair

proportion of the respondent's available income that should go to the support of the claimant.

(viii) Where the respondent's income comprises a base salary and a discretionary bonus the claimant's award may be equivalently partitioned, with needs of strict necessity being met from the base salary and additional, discretionary, items being met from the bonus on a capped percentage basis.

(ix) There is no criterion of exceptionality on an application to extend a term order. On such an application an examination should to be made of whether the implicit premise of the original order of the ability of the payee to achieve independence had been impossible to achieve and, if so, why.

(x) On an application to discharge a joint lives order an examination should be made of the original assumption that it was just too difficult to predict eventual independence.

(xi) If the choice between an extendable and a non-extendable term is finely balanced the decision should normally be in favour of the economically weaker party."

SS v NS concerned a relatively short 6-year marriage which produced three children, aged 11, 9 and 7. The wife had been a full-time mother throughout the marriage and the husband a banker. The husband had recently moved to a new banking job after having cancer and the wife was training to be a Pilates instructor, with minimal income. Mostyn J determined that the matrimonial assets of some £3.29m should be divided equally between the parties. On the question of maintenance, the court determined that the wife should receive 20% of the husband's bonuses for 6 years, £30,000 in spousal maintenance until the youngest child was 18 and an 'income top up' of £18,000 per year for two years until she was qualified as a Pilates instructor.

The short duration of a marriage is a factor in favour of a clean-break, with no order for maintenance or a short-term maintenance order only, particularly where there are no children of the family and both parties are working. This is because in shorter marriages there has been little time for financial dependence to grow between the parties, less time for needs to generate and less time for the parties to become accustomed to the standard of living enjoyed during the marriage. See Chapter 2 on needs, for a more in-depth analysis of needs in short marriage cases, above.

7.3 When will a maintenance order be made following a short marriage?

As Mostyn J said in *SS v NS*, the duration of the marriage and presence of children will often be the pivotal factors when it comes to considering an award for maintenance, along with the income disparity between the parties. In ***SS v NS***[196], Mostyn J considered the basis for long-term maintenance awards and stated:

> "*In Miller Baroness Hale at para 138 explained that the most common rationale for imposing the obligation to maintain into the future is to meet needs which the relationship has generated.* ***Obviously this is a very sound rationale and it is for this reason that the factors of duration of marriage and the birth of children are so important. It is hard to see how a relationship has generated needs in the case of a short childless marriage, although this is not impossible.*** *But where it can be argued that the relationship has generated hard needs why should meeting them be for longer than, say, the Scottish limit? The answer is best given by Lord Hope at para 118 where he explains why the Scottish limit is so unfair: "the career break which results from concentrating on motherhood and the family in the middle years of their lives comes at a price which in most cases is irrecoverable". For many women the marriage is the defining economic event of their*

[196] *(Spousal Maintenance)* [2014] EWHC 418 (Fam), paragraph 30.

> *whole lives and the decisions made in it may well reverberate for many years after its ending.*"

It is unusual for the court to make a maintenance award in a short marriage case unless children are present. If a maintenance award is made, it is likely to be made only to cover the short-term, while the financially-weaker party adjusts to independent life.

An example of a short childless marriage resulting in an award for maintenance is ***VV v VV***[197], in which, following a marriage of five months in which the parties lived an incredibly luxurious lifestyle, the wife who had only a negligible income of her own, was awarded £150,000 for three years (capitalised), by way of 'rehabilitative maintenance'. Relevant factors included the wife's financial dependence on the husband, which had commenced before the parties' marriage/cohabitation (with the husband giving the wife £117,000 in one year) and post-separation, with the husband providing the wife with £4,000 per month within proceedings. The husband was ordered to pay the wife's debts and redeem her mortgage. Overall, the wife was to receive £1.2m out of some £11.8m.

'Rehabilitative maintenance' was also ordered in ***MD v D***, which concerned a 4.5-year childless marriage. The wife was a newly qualified barrister, not earning enough at the time of the hearing to meet her stated needs of £38,000. The husband (a retired judge sitting part-time in retirement) was ordered to pay the wife £20,000 for the first year after the divorce, £15,000 in the second year and £10,000 in the third year, after which there would be a clean break. This approach was said to strike a balance between the husband's decreasing income and the wife's increasing income.

---

[197] [2022] EWFC 41, [2023] 1 FLR 170.

Another example of the court ordering spousal maintenance following a short childless marriage is ***FF v KF***[198], which concerned a 4.5 year marriage. This case was unusual on its facts as a result of the wife having a psychological breakdown, which impacted on her earning capacity and needs. W was awarded £1,341,500 as an income-producing fund at first instance. The husband's appeal was dismissed by Mostyn J, who noted that though generous, the income fund was not wrong, having regard to the extent of the husband's wealth, the wife's medical condition and the standard of living enjoyed during the marriage.

The majority of short marriage cases where the court has made a maintenance award involve the parties having at least one child. If there are no children, there will need to be some other need present to justify the maintenance order, such as financial dependence, minimal income or medical needs.

Once the court has decided to make a maintenance order, it must then determine the quantum of the maintenance ordered and the duration of the order.

7.4 Quantum of maintenance

There is clear authority for arguing that the duration of the marriage is relevant to the quantum of any maintenance order. In ***C v C***[199], Ward LJ said:

> "*(2) If there is to be no clean break, and a periodical payments order is to be made, then the court must decide pursuant to s 25 what amount is to be ordered. The duration of the marriage is a factor relevant to the determination of quantum.*"

---

[198] [2017] EWHC 1093 (Fam).

[199] *(financial relief: short marriage)* [1997] 2 FLR 26.

However, the duration of the marriage is just one factor for the court to consider alongside the income and assets available, the financial needs of the parties and the standard of living enjoyed during the marriage. Each case will turn on its specific facts.

7.5 For what duration should a maintenance order be made in short marriage cases?

In ***C v C***[200], a pre-***Miller*** case, Ward LJ giving the lead judgment in the Court of Appeal described the facts of the case as "highly unusual" and "unique". Following a marriage of just nine and a half months the wife was awarded secured periodical payments for the child and herself on a joint lives' basis. The judge at first instance was mindful of the brevity of the marriage and his duty to consider the marriage's duration, but noted that, although the marriage had been short, it had had profound consequences on the wife in terms of the impact of the breakdown of the marriage on her health and her commitment to the parties' child.

The husband appealed and argued that the periodical payments order was too high and that a term of 2-years was more appropriate. The Court of Appeal acknowledged that the maintenance award was high, however, could not fault the making of the joint lives maintenance order. Ward LJ outlined the following guidance to be considered by the court when determining whether to impose a term for a maintenance order:

> "*...(3) If a periodical payments order is made, whether for 5p pa or whatever, the question is whether it would be appropriate to impose a term because in the absence of such a direction the order will endure for joint lives or until the remarriage of the payee: see s 28(1)(a).*
>
> *(4) The statutory test is this: is it appropriate to order periodical payments only for such a term as in the opinion of the court would be*

[200] Ibid.

sufficient to enable the payee to adjust without undue hardship to the termination of financial dependence on the paying party?

(5) What is appropriate must of necessity depend on all the circumstances of the case including the welfare of any minor child and the s 25 checklist factors, one of which is the duration of the marriage. It is, however, not appropriate simply to say, "This is a short marriage, therefore a term must be imposed".

(6) Financial dependence being evident from the very making of an order for periodical payments, the question is whether, in the light of all the circumstances of the case, the payee can adjust – and adjust without undue hardship – to the termination of financial dependence and if so when. The question is, can she adjust, not should she adjust. In answering that question the court will pay attention not only to the duration of the marriage but to the effect the marriage and its breakdown and the need to care for any minor children has had and will continue to have on the earning capacity of the payee and the extent to which she is no longer in the position she would have been in but for the marriage, its consequences and its breakdown. It is highly material to consider any difficulties the payee may have in entering or re-entering the labour market, resuming a fractured career and making up any lost ground.

(7) The court cannot form its opinion that a term is appropriate without evidence to support its conclusion. Facts supported by evidence must, therefore, justify a reasonable expectation that the payee can and will become self-sufficient. Gazing into the crystal ball does not give rise to such a reasonable expectation. Hope, with or without pious exhortations to end dependency, is not enough.

(8) It is necessary for the court to form an opinion not only that the payee will adjust, but also that the payee will have adjusted within the term that is fixed. The court may be in a position of such certainty that it can impose a deferred clean break by prohibiting an extension of the term pursuant to s 28(1A). If, however, there is doubt about when self-

> *sufficiency will be attained, it is wrong to require the payee to apply to extend the term. If there is uncertainty about the appropriate length of the term, the proper course is to impose no term but leave the payer to seek the variation and if necessary go through the same exercise, this time pursuant to s 31(7)(a).*"

Due to the uncertainty as to the wife's future in relation to her health and earning capacity, the Court could not be satisfied that the wife could adjust without undue hardship at any point, and therefore it was not appropriate to impose a term for the maintenance award. ***C v C*** is therefore authority for the court making joint lives maintenance orders even following very short marriages, though note the unusual facts and the fact that the "mood music" in the family courts these days is very much against such orders being made.

Note that in ***G v G***[201], Charles J made clear that ***C v C***[202] needs to be read and applied in light of the significant changes introduced by ***Miller; McFarlane***[203] and the duty of the court to consider whether the initial order for periodical payments should:

> "*(a) take immediate account of the earnings and/or earning capacity of the payee; or*
>
> *(b) build in reductions to take account of them and so reduce rather than terminate financial dependence on the other spouse.*"[204]

In ***G v G***[205], the parties were married for five years and had one child, age 4. The wife had given up her career as a barrister to care for the parties'

201 [2012] EWHC 167 (Fam), [2012] 2 FLR 48.

202 *(financial relief: short marriage)* [1997] 2 FLR 26.

203 [2006] UKHL 24, [2006] 2 AC 618.

204 G v G [2012] EWHC 167 (Fam), [2012] 2 FLR 48, paragraph 141.

205 [2012] EWHC 167 (Fam), [2012] 2 FLR 48.

child and her caring responsibilities for the parties' child was the magnetic factor in the case. Charles J would not accept that the wife's future earning capacity was uncertain simply because the wife had failed to provide a report of her expected earnings. The court was satisfied the wife could and should work part-time while caring for the child. The husband was ordered to pay the wife £95,000 per annum in spousal maintenance, reducing to £75,000 per annum after 2 years, £55,000 per annum after 4 years and £35,000 per annum after 6 years, when the child would be 10. The £35,000 maintenance order was RPI-indexed for life.

In ***R v R***[206], in which the parties were married for 7 years, had two children and the husband's income was £186,000 per annum before any pool payment, the wife was awarded spousal maintenance of £55,000 per annum plus 20% of any pool payments received by the husband up to a maximum of £20,000. In considering the appropriate term for the periodical payments order, Coleridge explicitly considered the short duration of the marriage, noting:

> "*So now reverting to the question of a clean break on receipt of the deferred fund, I bear in mind that after a fairly short marriage, the wife's entitlement to continue to receive a very high income order long after separation is limited and I also make the reasonable prediction that the husband's income will fall considerably and eventually disappear in the years after he is 60.*"[207]

Coleridge J determined that on payment to the wife of a further lump sum of £650,000 from the eventual sale of the husband's property development enterprise, the periodical payments order would terminate and stand dismissed, as the lump sum would enable the wife to meet her ongoing needs.

---

206 [2011] EWHC 3093 (Fam), [2013] 1 FLR 120.

207 Ibid. paragraph 53.

In ***VV v VV***[208], in which there were no children and the wife was awarded £150,000 per year for three years by way of 'rehabilitative maintenance', Peel J made clear that a *Duxbury* award was not appropriate given the short duration of the marriage, and considered that maintenance for three years, which was a little longer than the duration of the parties' entire relationship, was appropriate. In short marriages without children, if maintenance is ordered at all, it is likely to be 'rehabilitative maintenance', i.e. a modest sum paid for a short time to enable to financially weaker party to resume their career.

In ***X v D***[209], HHJ Farquhar ordered that following a marriage of just four months which produced one child, the husband should pay the wife spousal periodical payments of £2,000 per month (in addition to child maintenance) until the parties' child finished full-time education, with a s28(1A) bar.

In ***UD v TQ***[210], HHJ Hess made an order for spousal maintenance of £2,000 per month (in addition to child maintenance) for a period of 3.5 years, after which payments would vary to a nominal level for 6.5 years, without a section 28(1A) bar.

Self-evidently there is a wide discretion available to the court as to the appropriate duration to make a spousal periodical payments order. As usual, the appropriate duration will depend on all the circumstances of the case, but in particular the resources available and the financially-weaker party's ability to adjust to independence without undue hardship.

---

[208] [2022] EWFC 41, [2023] 1 FLR 170.

[209] [2023] EWFC 332 (B).

[210] [2024] EWFC 119 (B).

CHAPTER EIGHT

PENSIONS IN A SHORT MARRIAGE CASE

8.1 Distinguishing needs and sharing cases

The Report of the Pension Advisory Group: A Guide to the Treatment of Pensions on Divorce (second edition) (January 2024) ("PAG 2") provides authoritative guidance on all areas of pensions, including the relevance of a marriage's duration to the court's approach to pensions.

One significant takeaway from PAG 2 when it comes to short marriages, is that the duration of the marriage is much more relevant in sharing cases than needs cases. The Pension Advisory Group state:

> "*In needs-based cases the timing and source of pension assets is not generally a relevant consideration as the court can have resort to any assets, whenever acquired, to ensure the parties' needs are met. In sharing cases the issue of timing, source and apportionment remains live.*"[211]

The court's approach is summarised by the Pension Advisory Group as follows:

> "*Thus, the court will have regard to the length of seamless cohabitation/marriage when determining the extent to which it is fair and reasonable to divide the 'non-matrimonial' element of any capital or any pension.*

---

[211] Report of the Pension Advisory Group: A Guide to the Treatment of Pensions on Divorce (second edition) (January 2024), page 3.

> *A marriage is a marriage, and it is the fact of a Divorce Final Order that gives jurisdiction to the court to determine whether there shall be a PSO and, if so, at what level.*
>
> *All cases will be determined upon their own facts. The 'marital' element of any pension will usually be shared equally. For the reasons set out above, in needs-based cases, the timing and source of the pension saving is not necessarily relevant, but the Court will nevertheless have regard to the length (or shortness) of the seamless cohabitation/marriage in determining the extent to which the needs of the claiming party will justify a division of the pre cohabitation/ marriage element of the pension…*"[212]

This means that in 'sharing cases', where the parties' assets exceed their assessed needs, the duration of the marriage is more relevant to pension-sharing than in 'needs' cases. In sharing cases, the court is more likely to consider whether any element of the parties' pensions was accrued prior to the marriage and is therefore non-matrimonial and not subject to equal sharing. If there is to be a pension sharing order at all, it will only be the element of the pension accrued during the marriage which is shared.

However, where the parties assets are insufficient to meet both of their needs, and both parties have retirement needs which need to be met, the court is unlikely to have regard to whether a pension was accrued before or during the marriage, and the parties' pensions may well be divided without regard to when the pension monies were accrued to provide both parties with the pension income required to meet their needs.

8.2 Needs cases

In short marriage 'needs' cases, pension sharing orders are relatively rare. When considering when it might be appropriate for there to be no pension sharing order, the Pension Advisory Group has given the

[212] Ibid., page 26 para 4.9-4.11.

example of a short marriage case with no children, where the parties have worked throughout the marriage on broadly similar terms[213]. The general view of the courts is that pensions are less relevant to needs in short marriages than in longer marriages.

In ***C v C***[214], a case in which the parties were married for 9.5 months, when considering the issues, Ward LJ stated the following under the leading, "*Loss of pension*":

> "*Again, given the short duration of the marriage this is not a factor of great significance even though, given his proximity to retirement, it might otherwise have been more material. It is not a surprise that it is not expressly mentioned by the judge save in his sweeping up.*"

In ***WD v MH***[215], a short marriage case in which the assets were minimal, there was no information available as to the value of the husband's pension. Recorder Rhys Taylor considered that it was not proportionate to delay the final hearing to gather information about the husband's pension given the shortness of the marriage. He stated:

> "*I am very mindful that each party is either at or very close to an age when they might legitimately hope to retire. The potential significant capital value of H's pensions, relative to other assets in the case, are not lost on me. However, I simply do not find it helpful to delve into this following a short marriage. It cannot usually be right that a wife can make a significant claim to her husband's pension after such a short marriage. Still less so when there has been a very long delay before claims are resolved by the court. Especially in circumstances when the parties appear to have agreed a settlement back in 2008.*"[216]

---

213 Ibid. page 28.

214 *(financial relief: short marriage)* [1997] 2 FLR 26.

215 [2022] EWFC 162 (B).

216 Paragraph 73d.iii.

8.2.1 Retirement needs must be relationship-generated

There is a suggestion within PAG 2 that parties seeking a pension sharing order following a short marriage case may have an additional hurdle to prove, in that they will need to establish that their need for retirement income is 'relationship-generated'. The Pension Advisory Group state:

> "*Short cohabitation/marriage cases may require consideration of whether any asserted need for retirement income is a 'relationship generated' need to justify invasion of an otherwise non Matrimonial asset. The requirement of a nexus between the relationship and a financial need to be met by a matrimonial claim has long been recognised by the case law.*"[217]

Examples of factors indicating retirement needs following short marriages include:

- The presence of children
- Parties' close to retirement age
- Large disparity in pension provision between the parties
- One party having less opportunity than the other to build up their pension pot before retirement, possibly due to one party having taken a career break during the marriage.

Note that more than one of the above factors are likely to be required for the court to consider that a pension should be shared to meet needs. For example, in ***RN v TT***[218], HHJ Hess considered that the husband had no

---

[217] Report of the Pension Advisory Group: A Guide to the Treatment of Pensions on Divorce (second edition) (January 2024), page 26 paras 4.9-4.11.

[218] [2024] EWFC 264.

relationship-generated needs after an 8-year marriage that produced two children in which the husband had no pension and the wife pensions worth some £600,000.

Once the court has decided that it is going to make a pension sharing order, it needs to consider the amount of pension monies that are required to be shared in order to meet the identified needs. The court will have regard to all of the circumstances of the case and the s 25 factors. In longer-marriage needs cases a pension sharing order providing for equality of pension income may be considered the court's starting point, but this is not the case for short marriages, when the court will consider how to meet the needs generated by the marriage.

8.2.2 Case examples

Pension Sharing Orders are relatively rare in short marriage 'needs' cases. The reported short marriage needs cases indicate that where a party has identifiable retirement needs following a short marriage, those needs are more likely to be met by way of an offsetting, maintenance, or provision of housing which may be downsized in the future to release capital. Examples of the court's approach to retirement needs in short marriage 'needs' cases are detailed below.

SS v NS (Spousal Maintenance)[219] is a rare example of the court making a pension sharing order following a relatively short 6-year marriage. Mostyn J ordered that the parties' pensions be divided equally between both parties. Relevant factors were that the marriage produced three children, the wife had been a full-time mother throughout the marriage and had minimal income, and that her capacity to contribute to her pension in the years until her retirement would be minimal.

---

219 [2014] EWHC 4183, [2015] 2 FLR 1124.

In ***M v L***[220], which was a Part III case, the parties were married for four years, had two children, and had been separated for 30 years before the court heard the wife's application. During the 30 years since separation, the wife had lived in a flat owned by the husband rent-free and received voluntary maintenance from the husband. At the time of the hearing the wife was 57 and the husband 64. The husband had assets of around £2.2m. The Court awarded the wife maintenance of £1,000 per month, capitalised at £150,000, to provide her with an income during her retirement.

In ***MD v D***[221], the parties had been married for 4.5 years and had no children. The wife was 52 and a newly-qualified barrister, the husband was 70 and a retired circuit judge sitting part-time in retirement. The total non-pension assets were £895,000. The wife had a pension worth just under £34,000 and the husband had pensions equivalent to around £660,000, which were already in payment. The first instance judge acknowledged that the wife had a need to build up her pension and awarded her the former family home with net equity of £287,400, on the basis that she would be over-housed and would be able to sell the family home and release some money for her pension in the future. This amounted to the wife receiving 37% of the non-pension assets, which the first instance just considered fair given the husband's contributions.

The wife appealed. Mark Potter P concluded that the judge's award left the wife with around £15,000 by way of pension provision, which was insufficient to meet her needs. Given the circumstances of the case, it was impractical to provide the wife with a pension that would meet her eventual needs, but given the available assets, a fair order would have been to provide the wife with £50,000 to kick-start her future pension. This would give the wife 41% of the non-pension assets. The husband was ordered to pay the wife an additional £35,000. It was noted that where there is insufficient assets to meet both parties' reasonable needs without

---

220 [2003] EWHC 328 (Fam).

221 [2008] EWHC 1929 (Fam) [2009] 1 FLR 810.

a substantial reduction in the expectations for both parties, the focus had to be on the parties' minimal future needs rather than on the distinction between the matrimonial and non-matrimonial property.

In two relatively short marriage cases, ***Fields v Fields***[222], which concerned an 8.5 year marriage, and ***AB v FC (Short Marriage: Needs: Stockpiling)***[223], which concerned a 19 month marriage, the court ordered the husbands to pay the wives maintenance which went over and above their income needs so that they could save or 'stockpile' for the future. In both cases it was suggested by the court that the stockpile fund should be used to fund a repayment mortgage so that the capital in the wives' homes could be accessed should they need it in the future. In ***Fields v Fields***, Holman J stated:

> *"Mr Marks submits that, as well as meeting her annual needs, payments must also be made to the wife to enable her (in his words) to "stockpile". He submits that, just as the husband has included £100,000 per annum in his budget under a heading "Pension", she needs to be able to make some similar provision of pension or stockpile for herself. In principle I accept and agree with that argument on the facts and in the circumstances of this particular case, having regard in particular to the respective ages of the husband, the wife and the children in relation to each other. If, however, there is an element of stockpile, it must of course be saved and in some way ring-fenced, so that it is indeed available for future needs and can be identified and taken into account if or when the husband's income drops and he seeks to reduce the level of periodical payments or discharge them altogether."*[224]

222 [2015] EWHC 1670 (Fam), [2016] 1 FLR 1186.

223 [2016] EWHC 3285 (Fam), [2017] 4 WLR 35.

224 Fields v Fields [2015] EWHC 1670 (Fam), [2016] 1 FLR 1186, paragraph 56.

8.3 Sharing cases

In sharing cases, the starting point is that the court will share equally pension funds which have accrued during the marriage and are therefore matrimonial. The date from which accrued pension funds are matrimonial is the date of cohabitation as opposed to marriage[225]. It is arguable whether monies accrued post-separation will count as matrimonial or not, with some authorities suggesting that assets accruing post-separation will not be subject to sharing[226] and others suggesting that assets accrued in the 12 months after separation may be shared[227].

Where questions arise as to the apportionment of a pension according to the period of the marriage, a Pension On Divorce Expert (PODE) should always be instructed to advise on the value of the pension that was accrued during the marriage. The Pension Advisory Group advise that PODEs should be given clear instructions as to how their calculation should be carried out. They should be instructed to use one of the following methods[228]:

- Deferred pension method - PODE accounts for passive growth on pension monies accrued before and during the marriage.

- Cash Equivalent method - PODE compares the cash equivalent value of the pension at the end of the marriage compared with

---

225 *GW v RW* [2003] EWHC 611 (Fam); *Co v Co* (Ancillary Relief – Pre-Marriage Cohabitation) [2004] 1FLR 1095; *M v M* (Financial Relief – Substantial Earning Capacity) [2004] 2 FLR 236.

226 See Waggott v Waggott [2018] EWCA Cuv 727 and C v C [2019] 1 FLR 939.

227 See Rossi v Rossi [2001] 1 FLR 790 and E v L [2021] EWFC 60.

228 See Report of the Pension Advisory Group: A Guide to the Treatment of Pensions on Divorce (second edition) (January 2024), page 26 para 4.9-4.11, Part 12 & Appendix S.

the cash equivalent value of the pension at the date cohabitation commenced.

- Straight-line method – PODE assumes pension benefits have accrued evenly over the period that the pension fund has been contributed to.

The Pension Advisory Group recommend that pensions should be assessed and divided as an asset class of their own, separately from other capital assets[229]. In ***SP v AL (PL and another intervening)***[230], HHJ Hess considered the guidance in PAG 2 and noted:

> "***In seeking fairness in relation to the division of pensions should the court, if possible, disaggregate the pensions in the case and promote a discrete and fair division of the pensions as opposed to attempting to execute an offset against other assets?*** *The orthodox view, encouraged by Thorpe LJ in Martin-Dye v Martin-Dye [2006] 2 FLR 901, is that pensions should be dealt with separately and discretely from other capital assets. The PAG 2 Report offers a similar view: "try, if possible, to deal with each asset class in isolation and avoid offsetting - a discrete solution which equalises pensions by pension sharing orders and which equalises non-pension assets by lump sum or property adjustment orders" (page 42). Sometimes the facts of a case mean that an off-setting solution has to be followed, but if it can be avoided, as in the present case, that is generally desirable.*"

In ***SP v AL***[231], HHJ Hess considered a marriage which he found was 9 years in duration. The husband was 57 and the wife 50. The wife had an NHS pension with CE £345,900 and the husband had an NHS pension with CE £1,513,000 and prudential pension with CE £20,515. When

229 Ibid. pages 41-42.

230 [2024] EWFC 72 (B), paragraph 39.

231 Ibid.

considering whether and what proportion of the husband's pensions should be shared, HHJ Hess stated:

> "*In the present case, involving a medium length marriage in more mature years, where the parties have entered the marriage with significant assets acquired earlier in their adult lives, and where the case in terms of pension income sits more easily in the category of a 'sharing case' (the wife has not argued that she should have more based on a need claim), the fair answer is likely to be provided by focusing on a division of the pensions accrued in the span of the marriage's duration, that is to exclude the sharing of pensions outside this category on the basis that they represent non-matrimonial property. The report by Mr Conlon in this case has been targeted towards identifying the mathematical consequences of this principle and its conclusions should therefore be followed in the search for fairness.*"[232]

HHJ Hess ordered that 9.2% of the husband's NHS pension should be shared with the wife, that representing the figure needed to produce equal income on retirement for the parties, having regard only to the pension funds accrued over the 9 years of the marriage.

In ***E v L***[233], the parties were married for 3 years and 9 months. Mostyn J determined that the wife should receive half of all of the matrimonial assets, including the £67,115 worth of pension monies contributed by the husband to his pension during the period of the marriage.

In ***JS v RS***[234], the parties were in their forties, married for 6 years and had no children. The non-pension assets were £6.9m, the wife had a pension of £800,000 and the husband a pension of £140,000. Peter Singer J awarded the husband an additional £60,000 lump sum to offset the difference between the funds he contributed to his pension during the

[232] Ibid. para 40.

[233] [2021] EWFC 60, [2022] 1 FLR 952.

[234] [2024] EWFC 264 (B).

marriage and the funds the wife contributed to her pension during the marriage. Note that ***JS v RS*** was appealed as ***Sharp v Sharp***[235], but the appeal did not concern the decision in relation to pension off-setting.

In ***RN v TT***[236], the parties were married for 8 years, the wife was 51 and the husband 49. The husband had delayed for 9 years after separation before he made his application to court. The wife had pensions totalling £595,214 and the husband had no pension. On a sharing basis, HHJ Hess considered that the husband's award should be limited a lump sum of £35,000 which the wife offered, and a pension sharing order for 100% of the wife's Aviva pension (£107,347), which was roughly equivalent to half the value of the pension accrued during the marriage.

235 [2017] EWCA Civ 408.

236 [2024] EWFC 264 (B).

CHAPTER NINE

AGREEMENTS IN A SHORT MARRIAGE CASE

The agreements referred to in this section include prenuptial agreements (PNAs), post-nuptial agreements, separation agreements and any other agreements intended to be binding between two spouses. Agreements may be entered into by spouses before or after their marriage or at the point of separation, recording their intentions in the event that their relationship ends.

Agreements not included in court orders are not formally binding in England and Wales, but may be regarded by the court as persuasive or even decisive, depending on the circumstances in which the parties entered into the agreement and those prevailing at the time the relevance or weight to be attached to the agreement is being considered.

9.1 How does the court approach PNAs?

The duration of a marriage in and of itself has no bearing on the weight to be attached to an agreement reached between spouses. The court will consider whether it is fair to hold the parties to their agreement in the circumstances of each individual case. The main reason a court is likely to depart from the terms of an agreement is to ensure that the reasonable needs of the parties and any children of the family are provided for. The longer the marriage, the less likely it is that the parties will have planned for the marriage's breakdown in a manner that meets both parties' needs at the time of their eventual separation, having regard to the standard of living enjoyed during the marriage. There is an argument therefore that agreements made in anticipation of marriages which turn out to be short are more likely to be upheld because they are more likely to be fair to the parties, than PNAs made at the commencement of longer marriages.

The most significant case dealing with agreements is ***Radmacher (formerly Granatino) v Granatino***[237], in which the Supreme Court significantly increased the weight to be attached to PNAs. Before ***Radmacher***, PNAs were frequently considered to be non-binding, a 'relevant factor' or, at most, a 'magnetic factor'. ***Radmacher*** established the presumption that:

> "*75. … the court should give effect to a nuptial agreement that is freely entered into by each party with a full appreciation of its implications unless in the circumstances prevailing it would not be fair to hold the parties to their agreement.*"

In ***Radmacher*** at first instance Baron J considered it appropriate to ignore a PNA completely because no negotiations had taken place, the husband had not received independent legal advice, there was no disclosure by the wife and the agreement deprived the husband of all claims, in the context of children having be born of the marriage[238]. The Court of Appeal considered that Baron J was correct to conclude that the PNA was not enforceable but failed to give sufficient weight to the PNA by awarding the husband more than he needed to meet his role as a father and homemaker[239].

The Supreme Court considered that the husband should be held to the terms of the PNA, which he had freely entered into with an understanding of its consequences. The court determined that independent legal advice and full disclosure are not pre-requisites for a PNA to be effective. A prenuptial or postnuptial agreement will carry full

---

[237] [2010] UKSC 42.

[238] *NG v KR (Pre-Nuptial Contract)* [2008] EWHC 1532 (Fam).

[239] *Radmacher v Granatino* [2009] EWCA Civ 649.

weight if both parties enter into it of their own free will, without any undue influence or pressure and are informed of its implications.

Baroness Hale dissented from the view of the majority in ***Radmacher***[240], expressing reservations regarding the presumption that the parties be held to their pre-marital agreement. She stated that the guiding principle should be fairness in the light of the actual circumstances at the time when the court comes to make its decision, as opposed to those envisaged before the parties' marriage.

Radmacher[241] concerned a short-medium length marriage of 8 years. Notably, the Supreme Court placed no weight on the duration of the Radmacher marriage when it came to upholding the PNA, and made no general connection between the length of the marriage and the weight to be attached to a PNA, save for a reference to the earlier case of ***Crossley v Crossley***[242].

Crossley[243] concerned a marriage of very short duration between parties with substantial independent wealth and no children. The Court of Appeal upheld the first instance judge's decision to require the wife to show cause why her claim for ancillary relief should not be dealt with in accordance with the parties' pre-nuptial agreement. Thorpe LJ considered the pre-nuptial agreement was a factor of 'magnetic importance' in light of the exceptional combination of factors in the case including the short marriage, the parties living apart for much of the marriage, the parties both being mature adults with previous experience of marriage and divorce, the pre-nuptial agreement providing for both parties to retain their own property, and both parties having their own substantial wealth.

---

240 [2010] UKSC 42.

241 Ibid.

242 [2007] EWCA Civ 1491, [2008] 1 FCR 323.

243 Ibid.

In ***Radmacher***[244], the Supreme Court was clear that the court may reduce the weight attached to a PNA where factors such as duress, fraud or misrepresentation apply, or where the agreement is clearly unfair having regard to the circumstances prevailing at the time of the marriage breakdown.

When considering the weight to be attached to a PNA, the court will carry out a two-stage exercise:

(1) are there any circumstances surrounding the making of the PNA which should eliminate or reduce the weight to be attached to the agreement?

(2) does the PNA operate fairly now having regard to all of the section 25 factors including the marital standard of living and needs?

Examples of where the court has not upheld agreements include:

- the PNA does not meet the needs of the financially-weaker party or the parties' children[245];

- one party did not appreciate the implications of the agreement, the agreement was the product of pressure by the other party and there was a material absence of legal advice or disclosure[246];

244 [2010] UKSC 42.

245 e.g. *Kremen v Agrest (No 11) (Financial Remedy: Non-Disclosure: Post-Nuptial Agreement)* [2012] EWHC 45 (Fam).

246 Ibid.

- the PNA anticipated the parties would be living in Scandinavia, when they were in fact living in England, and made no provision for maintenance[247];

- the agreement was unfair in that it made inadequate provision for one party's needs, providing the husband with about 95% of the assets and the wife only about 5%[248];

- the PNA was signed the day before the wedding[249] or 5 days before the wedding "*where no advice had been given or disclosure exchanged*"[250];

- the PNA made no provision at all for the economically-weaker party[251];

- the PNA was not in the parties' first language[252];

Examples of where agreements have been upheld even where potentially vitiating factors have been present include:

---

[247] *AH v PH (Scandinavian Marriage Settlement)* [2013] EWHC 3873 (Fam).

[248] *DB v PB (Financial Provision) (Prenuptial Agreement: Prorogation Clause)* [2016] EWHC 3431 (Fam).

[249] *AD v BD (Financial Remedies)* [2020] EWHC 857 (Fam) and *D v D (Financial Remedies: Pre-marital agreement and Unequal Shares)* [2020] EWHC 857 (Fam).

[250] *S v H* [2020] EWFC B16.

[251] see Moor J in *IR v OR* [2022] EWFC 20 and Mostyn J in *Ipekci v McConnell* [2019] EWFC 19.

[252] *XW v XH (Financial Remedies: Non-Matrimonial Assets)* [2017] EWFC 76.

- there was pressure on one party to enter the agreement, but the pressure did not amount to *undue* pressure[253];

- one party made clear that there would be no marriage without the other party entering into a PNA - this is not sufficient to amount to undue pressure[254];

- a PNA was signed the day before the wedding in Sweden, where such agreements are commonplace, simply drafted and generally signed without legal advice or disclosure[255];

- there had not been independent legal advice or full disclosure, but the marriage contract was entered into in France, where such contracts are commonplace[256];

- the PNA was signed on the wedding day but the parties had had around a month to consider and amend the document and take legal advice, had they wished to[257].

The court will depart from the terms of a PNA where the PNA is not fair, and particularly where it does not adequately meet one of the party's needs (and there are assets available to meet both parties' needs). Holman J summarised the approach that the court should take when considering whether a PNA is fair in ***Luckwell v Limata***[258]:

---

253 *WC v HC (Financial Remedies Agreements)* [2022] EWFC 22, per Peel J at [36].

254 *MN v AN (Prenuptial Agreement)* [2023] EWHC 613 (Fam), per Moor J at [80].

255 *Versteegh v Versteegh* [2018] EWCA Civ 1050.

256 *CMX v EJX (French Marriage Contract)* [2022] EWFC 136.

257 *HD v WB* [2023] EWFC 2.

258 [2014] EWHC 502 (Fam) at [130].

> *"Whether it will 'not be fair to hold the parties to the agreement' will necessarily depend on the facts, but some guidance can be given:*
>
> *i) A nuptial agreement cannot be allowed to prejudice the reasonable requirements of any children;*
>
> *ii) Respect for autonomy, including a decision as to the manner in which their financial affairs should be regulated, may be particularly relevant where the agreement addresses the existing circumstances and not merely the contingencies of an uncertain future;*
>
> *iii) There is nothing inherently unfair in an agreement making provision dealing with existing non-marital property including anticipated future receipts, and there may be good objective justifications for it, such as obligations towards family members;*
>
> *iv) The longer the marriage has lasted the more likely it is that events have rendered what might have seemed fair at the time of making the agreement unfair now, particularly if the position is not as envisaged;*
>
> *v) It is unlikely to be fair that one party is left in a predicament of real need while the other has 'a sufficiency or more';*
>
> *vi) Where each party is able to meet his or her needs, fairness may well not require a departure from the agreement."*

The case law suggests that there is a greater risk that PNA's will be unfair in longer marriages than shorter marriages. In a shorter marriage, there will have been less time for the parties' circumstances to change and less time for the parties to become accustomed to the standard of living enjoyed during the marriage, than in longer marriages. In ***HD v WB***[259], Peel J explicitly stated that the duration of the parties' cohabitation was one of the reasons that he considered it unfair to hold the husband to the PNA, noting that the PNA failed to meet the husband's housing or

[259] [2023] EWFC 2.

income needs "*in a way which bears at least some relation to the marital lifestyle enjoyed over some 20 years*".

Where there are no vitiating factors and the court departs from a PNA only to alleviate any unfairness, the PNA will still be afforded weight and the financially-weaker party's claim will usually be confined to meeting their reasonable needs. In these circumstances, the financially-weaker party's needs are likely to be assessed more conservatively than if there had been no agreement. Where the marriage has been short, and there has been a valid agreement, needs are likely to be assessed even more conservatively.

9.2 Short marriage cases

Examples of short marriage cases involving agreements are ***MB v EB***[260], ***Helliwell v Entwistle***[261], ***AH v BH***[262] and ***WD v MH***[263].

In ***MB v EB***[264] the parties were married for 4 years between 2000 and 2004. They executed a separation agreement in 2011 and the husband issues divorce proceedings in 2017. There were no marital assets, with the wife's wealth emanating from her family. The husband argued that vitiating factors, including duress, invalidated the 2011 separation agreement, and, alternatively, that it would be unfair to hold him to the agreement because holding him to it would leave him in a predicament of real need. Applying the principles in ***Radmacher***[265] Cohen J found that the agreement was valid, save that it may not meet the income needs

260 [2019] EWHC 1649 2 FLR 899.

261 [2024] EWHC 740 (Fam).

262 [2024] EWFC 125.

263 [2022] EWFC 162 (B).

264 [2019] EWHC 1649 2 FLR 899.

265 *Radmacher v Granatino* [2010] UKSC 42

of the husband. In considering the alleged vitiating factors, Cohen J noted that it was the husband who had initiated the process leading up to the agreement being executed, with the terms of the agreement reflected the husband's own proposals. There was no evidence that the wife pressurised the husband or exploited her dominant position and as such, the vitiating factors were not made out. Although disclosure was not mutually exchanged, the husband was aware that the wife came from a wealthy family and as such, nothing more was needed in terms of disclosure.

In ***Helliwell v Entwistle***[266], the parties were married for three years. The wife had assets of £61.5m-£74m and the husband had assets of £850,000, £500,000 of which was tied up in a property in Spain. The husband originally sought £10m and by the time of trial sought £2.4m. The wife offered the husband nothing, in accordance with the PNA they had signed. Francis J upheld the PNA which prevented sharing and limited the husband's award to his reasonable needs. Bearing the PNA in mind, Francis J considered it would be wrong to require the wife to provide funds to enable the husband to purchase a property, and awarded the husband a total of £455,000 to cover two years of rent, the purchase of a car and maintenance for two years, while he increased his earning capacity. Undoubtedly the husband's needs-based award would have been higher absent the PNA.

In ***AH v BH***[267], Peel J considered that following a 5.5 year marriage which produced two children, a PNA was unfair because it failed to provide adequately for the wife and children. In particular, the PNA stated that it would be reviewed following the birth of any children of the marriage, but had not been, indicating that the parties contemplated that the PNA might not be a fair document upon children being born. There were assets of £50m and the wife was awarded £3.05m for a housing fund and £710,000 worth of capitalised maintenance, in addition to child

266 [2024] EWHC 740 (Fam).

267 [2024] EWFC 125.

maintenance. Including her own assets of c.£292,000, the wife's total assets at the end of the marriage were just 8% of the total assets. Peel J noted that if it were not for the PNA, the wife's needs award would have been greater and she may have been entitled to additional funds on a sharing basis. Although the wife's needs were assessed conservatively, Peel J rejected the husband's argument that the wife's housing should be provided for on a Schedule 1 basis (reverting to the husband after the children finished tertiary education), stating at paragraph 53:

> "*It is of note that, so far as I am aware, there is not a single reported PMA case where a primary carer of the children, with no significant assets of his/her own, has not received a sum of money for housing outright.*"

In ***WD v MH***[268], the parties had separated following short marriage and reached a financial agreement recorded in a consent order and approved by a District Judge in 2008. The agreement provided either for the wife to take over the mortgage on the family home and pay the husband £25,000, or for the husband to retain the family home and pay the wife £30,000 (50% of the value of the equity). The wife did not buy-out H's share and the agreement was not fully implemented. The consent order was never made into an enforceable order as no decree was made in the parties' judicial separation proceedings. Upon dismissal of the judicial separation proceedings in 2019, the status of 2008 agreement morphed into a post-nuptial marital agreement, entered into with the assistance of solicitors.

At the final hearing, the husband sought to implement the 2008 agreement, offering the wife £30,000. The wife sought for the family home to be transferred to her or sold, with the husband's equity divided equally between them, providing her with £250,000-£300,000. Recorder Rhys Taylor considered that the figure of £30,000 in the 2008 agreement should be uplifted to reflect the time that had passed to £60,000, but

[268] [2022] EWFC 162 (B).

otherwise upheld the agreement. He considered that wife was able to meet her conservatively assessed needs without recourse to the husband's funds in circumstances where she was living in a council property and claiming benefits. The magnetic factors in that case were the shortness of the marriage, the 2008 agreement and the wife's delay of some 13 years in bringing an application for financial remedies.

CHAPTER TEN

CONCLUSION

The treatment of short marriages within financial remedy proceedings remains a nuanced and evolving area of family law. This book has explored the manner in which the court will assess financial claims in short marriages, distinguishing them from longer unions where financial entanglements and interdependencies are more pronounced.

The application of s.25 of the Matrimonial Causes Act 1973 gives judges broad discretion, leading to potential variation in outcomes. The unpredictable nature of financial remedy cases means that similar factual circumstances can yield different outcomes.

The legal landscape surrounding short marriages continues to evolve, with growing judicial recognition of modern relationship dynamics, including pre-marital cohabitation, career sacrifices, and financial autonomy. The court's role is to balance fairness with financial independence, ensuring that parties can move forward without undue hardship while respecting the contributions made during the marriage.

For family law practitioners, understanding the nuances of short marriage financial remedy cases is essential. Whether advising clients on financial settlements or drafting prenuptial agreements, a strategic and well-informed approach is key to securing the best possible outcome.

Summary

The Definition and Relevance of Short Marriages

The absence of a statutory definition means the court relies on case law to determine what qualifies as a "short marriage," with marriages under five years generally considered short. Judicial discretion plays a crucial role, in some cases treating marriages of six to seven years as short, depending on the level of financial entanglement.

How the Court Assesses the Duration of Marriage

Pre-marital cohabitation forms part of the overall relationship duration, if it flows seamlessly into marriage. Similarly, post-separation financial ties can extend the court's assessment of when a marriage has ended.

Needs

Needs are likely to take precedence over sharing in short marriage cases because there will have been less time for matrimonial assets to accumulate, and a needs award is likely to be smaller than a sharing-award.

Needs are assessed more conservatively following a short marriage than a long marriage, as there will have been less time for financial interdependence to grow and relationship-based needs to generate. The court's goal is to ensure fairness while avoiding disproportionate awards that do not reflect the brevity of the relationship.

Sharing

In ***Miller v Miller***, Lord Nicholls confirmed that equal sharing applies to all marriages, regardless of duration, but that the short duration of a marriage will naturally limit the size of the matrimonial pot. In short and long marriages alike, the sharing principle requires the court to divide the matrimonial assets between the parties.

In short marriage cases, non-matrimonial assets are likely to be excluded unless they are required to meet needs. The court recognises that a party who enters a short marriage with significant pre-acquired wealth should not necessarily be required to share it upon divorce.

Non-matrimonial property plays a significant role in financial remedy cases involving short marriages. Unlike long-term unions, where non-matrimonial assets may become intertwined with shared finances, short marriages often allow clearer distinctions between matrimonial and non-matrimonial assets because there has been less time for the mingling and matrimonialisation of pre-acquired assets. As a result, the court is generally more inclined to ring-fence non-matrimonial property, ensuring that assets acquired before the marriage, through inheritance, or by gift remain

For family law practitioners, understanding the nuances of non-matrimonial property is essential, particularly when advising clients on asset protection, pre-nuptial agreements, and the strategic presentation of financial claims. Ultimately, while fairness remains the guiding principle, non-matrimonial wealth is less likely to be shared in short marriage cases, reinforcing the idea that financial obligations should reflect the limited duration of the relationship.

Clean Break Considerations

Given the court's duty under section 25A of the Matrimonial Causes Act 1973 to consider a clean break, most short marriages result in lump sum payments rather than ongoing financial support. Where assets are limited, the court may adjust a sharing claim downward to reflect the brevity of the marriage and the goal of financial independence. The court aims to ensure fairness by providing a transition to independence for the financially weaker spouse, while avoiding excessive awards that do not reflect the limited duration of the marriage

In short marriage needs cases, the court's primary focus is to ensure a fair transition to independent living. The standard of living during the marriage is relevant but does not necessarily dictate financial awards, particularly in very short marriages where dependency has not been established.

The Presence of Children

The presence of children in a short marriage significantly alters the court's approach to needs in short marriage cases. While the duration of the marriage is a key factor in determining financial awards, the welfare of any children remains the court's first consideration, as mandated by section 25 of the Matrimonial Causes Act 1973. This means that even in very short marriages, financial provisions may be substantial if required to meet the needs of a child and the primary carer.

The court will prioritize housing and maintenance needs for the primary carer to ensure the child has a stable home and standard of living. This overrides the usual reluctance to make significant financial awards in short marriages, as the child's well-being takes precedence over the brevity of the relationship. ***B v B***[269] and ***X v D***[270] highlight instances where the non-primary carer was required to provide a lump sum to secure housing for the child's primary residence.

The use of *Mesher* orders, where property ownership remains shared but sale is deferred until the child reaches adulthood, may be considered, but is not always appropriate.

While spousal maintenance is uncommon in short marriages, the presence of children can justify longer-term financial support for the primary carer. The court may order term-limited spousal maintenance, especially if the primary carer of the child has sacrificed career opportunities in order to care for the child. In ***Murphy v Murphy***[271],

[269] *(Mesher Order)*[2002] EWHC 3106 (Fam), [2003] 2 FLR 285.

[270] [2023] EWFC 332 (B)

[271] [2014] EWHC 2263, paragraph 35.

Holman J emphasized that having children "changes everything," and maintenance should reflect the caregiving responsibilities post-divorce.

Although clean breaks are favoured in short marriages, they may not be feasible where young children are involved. The need to provide for the child's upbringing and the primary carer's ability to support themselves often leads to longer-term financial ties between the parties.

The court will consider that children require stability post-divorce, even if this means financial arrangements extend well beyond what would be expected in a short marriage without children. Ultimately, where children are involved, financial claims extend beyond the marriage itself and are shaped by the court's paramount duty to protect the best interests of the child.

Spousal Maintenance

Spousal maintenance in short marriages is generally limited in duration and scope, reflecting the principle that a brief union should not create long-term financial obligations. Unlike longer marriages, where one spouse may have become financially dependent on the other, short marriages typically involve fewer economic sacrifices and less financial entanglement. As a result, the court takes a cautious approach to awarding ongoing maintenance and prefer to achieve a clean break where possible.

In cases involving short marriages, the primary purpose of spousal maintenance is to assist the financially weaker party in transitioning to independent living. As established in ***Miller v Miller; McFarlane v McFarlane***[272], the objective is to provide a "gentle transition" rather than ongoing financial support over many years. The court is reluctant to

[272] [2006] UKHL 24, [2006] 2 AC 618.

order long-term maintenance, unless there are exceptional circumstances, such as disability or the presence of young children.

In many cases, term-limited maintenance (often referred to as rehabilitative maintenance) is awarded to allow the financially weaker spouse time to re-establish themselves.

Where both parties are financially self-sufficient, maintenance is unlikely to be awarded. In cases where one party has substantial pre-marital wealth, the court may resist long-term maintenance claims, especially if the marriage was too short for financial dependency to develop. ***McCartney v Mills McCartney***[273] demonstrated that even in high-net-worth cases, maintenance is assessed based on reasonable needs rather than indefinite support.

The case law indicates that short marriages rarely justify lifetime support.

Section 25A of the Matrimonial Causes Act 1973 places a duty on courts to consider a clean break wherever possible. In short marriages, the clean break principle is favoured, as it allows both parties to move forward without ongoing financial ties.

Advising clients on spousal maintenance in short marriages requires a pragmatic approach, ensuring that claims are realistic and supported by financial need rather than an expectation of long-term support. While maintenance remains a factor in short marriage financial settlements, it is not the norm, and where possible, courts will prioritize independence over continued financial reliance.

Pensions

Unlike long marriages, where pension assets are often a key component of financial settlements, short marriages typically involve limited or no

[273] [2008] EWHC 401 (Fam), [2008] 1 FLR 1508.

pension sharing. This is because in a short marriage, there is usually insufficient time for meaningful financial interdependence to develop between the parties.

Courts generally distinguish between pre-marital pension contributions (non-matrimonial) and contributions made during the marriage (matrimonial). In most short marriages, the portion of pension accrued during the relationship is relatively small and it is more appropriate to consider sharing pensions by way of off-setting than by pension sharing orders.

In in short marriages, the court's focus is on meeting the parties' immediate as opposed to long-term needs. The court is more likely to consider pension division where there is significant financial disparity, particularly if one party is close to retirement age and the other has little or no pension provision, or one party would face financial hardship without a pension sharing order.

Ultimately, while pension claims may arise in short marriage financial proceedings, they are rarely the central focus and will typically be secondary to housing and income needs.

Agreements

The duration of a marriage in and of itself has no bearing on the weight to be attached to a pre-nuptial agreement or other agreement reached between spouses. The case law indicates that pre-nuptial agreements are less likely to be departed from in short marriage cases than long ones because there will have been less time over the course of a short marriage for the parties' circumstances to change and the terms of the agreement to become unfair.

When advising clients before marriage, it may well be worth advising them to enter into a pre-nuptial agreement to avoid a sharing claim and avoid the uncertainties which would loom on marital breakdown.

'The Electronic Communications Code: A Practical Guide – Second Edition' by Kerry Bretherton KC, James Castle, Mark Loveday
'A Practical Guide to the Independent School Standards – September 2023 Edition' by Sarah McKimm
'A Practical Guide to Estate Administration and Crypto Assets' by Richard Marshall
'A Practical Guide to Parental Alienation in Private and Public Law Children Cases' by Sam King QC & Frankie Shama
'Contested Heritage – Removing Art from Land and Historic Buildings' by Richard Harwood QC, Catherine Dobson, David Sawtell
'The Limits of Separate Legal Personality: When Those Running a Company Can Be Held Personally Liable for Losses Caused to Third Parties Outside of the Company' by Dr Mike Wilkinson
'A Practical Guide to Transgender Law' by Robin Moira White & Nicola Newbegin
'A Practical Guide to 'Stranded Spouses' in Family Law' by Mani Singh Basi
'A Practical Guide to Residential Freehold Conveyancing' by Lorraine Richardson
'A Practical Guide to Pensions on Divorce for Lawyers' by Bryan Scant
'A Practical Guide to Challenging Sham Marriage Allegations in Immigration Law' by Priya Solanki
'A Practical Guide to Digital Communications Evidence in Criminal Law' by Sam Willis
'A Practical Guide to Legal Rights in Scotland' by Sarah-Jane Macdonald
'A Practical Guide to New Build Conveyancing' by Paul Sams & Rebecca East
'A Practical Guide to Inherited Wealth on Divorce' by Hayley Trim
'A Practical Guide to Practice Direction 12J and Domestic Abuse in Private Law Children Proceedings' by Rebecca Cross & Malvika Jaganmohan
'A Practical Guide to Confiscation and Restraint' by Narita Bahra QC, John Carl Townsend, David Winch
'A Practical Guide to the Law of Forests in Scotland' by Philip Buchan
'A Practical Guide to Health and Medical Cases in Immigration Law' by Rebecca Chapman & Miranda Butler
'A Practical Guide to Bad Character Evidence for Criminal Practitioners by Aparna Rao
'A Practical Guide to Extradition Law post-Brexit' by Myles Grandison et al
'A Practical Guide to Hoarding and Mental Health for Housing Lawyers' by Rachel Coyle

'Stephens on Contractual Indemnities' by Richard Stephens
'A Practical Guide to the EU Succession Regulation' by Richard Frimston
'A Practical Guide to Solicitor and Client Costs – Second Edition' by Robin Dunne
'Constructive Dismissal – Practice Pointers and Principles' by Benjimin Burgher
'A Practical Guide to Religion and Belief Discrimination Claims in the Workplace' by Kashif Ali
'A Practical Guide to the Law of Medical Treatment Decisions' by Ben Troke
'Fundamental Dishonesty and QOCS in Personal Injury Proceedings: Law and Practice' by Jake Rowley
'A Practical Guide to the Law in Relation to School Exclusions' by Charlotte Hadfield & Alice de Coverley
'A Practical Guide to Divorce for the Silver Separators' by Karin Walker
'The Right to be Forgotten – The Law and Practical Issues' by Melissa Stock
'A Practical Guide to Planning Law and Rights of Way in National Parks, the Broads and AONBs' by James Maurici QC, James Neill et al
'A Practical Guide to Election Law' by Tom Tabori
'A Practical Guide to the Law in Relation to Surrogacy' by Andrew Powell
'A Practical Guide to Claims Arising from Fatal Accidents – Second Edition' by James Patience
'A Practical Guide to Asbestos Claims' by Jonathan Owen & Gareth McAloon
'A Practical Guide to Stamp Duty Land Tax in England and Northern Ireland' by Suzanne O'Hara
'A Practical Guide to the Law of Farming Partnerships' by Philip Whitcomb
'A Practical Guide to the Law of Unlawful Eviction and Harassment – Second Edition' by Stephanie Lovegrove
'A Practical Guide to Costs in Personal Injury Claims – Second Edition' by Matthew Hoe
'A Practical Guide to the General Data Protection Regulation (GDPR) – Second Edition' by Keith Markham
'A Practical Guide to Working with Litigants in Person and McKenzie Friends in Family Cases' by Stuart Barlow
'Protecting Unregistered Brands: A Practical Guide to the Law of Passing Off' by Lorna Brazell
'A Practical Guide to Secondary Liability and Joint Enterprise Post-Jogee' by Joanne Cecil & James Mehigan

'A Practical Guide to the Pre-Action RTA Claims Protocol for Personal Injury Lawyers' by Antonia Ford

'A Practical Guide to Neighbour Disputes and the Law' by Alexander Walsh

'A Practical Guide to Coercive Control for Legal Practitioners and Victims' by Rachel Horman

'A Practical Guide to the Law of Driverless Cars – Second Edition'

by Alex Glassbrook, Emma Northey & Scarlett Milligan

'A Practical Guide to TOLATA Claims' by Greg Williams

'A Practical Guide to Elderly Law – Second Edition' by Justin Patten

'A Practical Guide to Responding to Housing Disrepair and Unfitness Claims' by Iain Wightwick

'A Practical Guide to the Law of Bullying and Harassment in the Workplace' by Philip Hyland

'How to Be a Freelance Solicitor: A Practical Guide to the SRA-Regulated Freelance Solicitor Model' by Paul Bennett

'A Practical Guide to Prison Injury Claims' by Malcolm Johnson

'A Practical Guide to Advising Clients at the Police Station' by Colin Stephen McKeown-Beaumont

'A Practical Guide to Antisocial Behaviour Injunctions – Second Edition' by Iain Wightwick

'Practical Mediation: A Guide for Mediators, Advocates, Advisers, Lawyers, and Students in Civil, Commercial, Business, Property, Workplace, and Employment Cases' by Jonathan Dingle with John Sephton

'The Mini-Pupillage Workbook' by David Boyle

'A Practical Guide to Crofting Law' by Brian Inkster

'A Practical Guide to the Law of Domain Names and Cybersquatting' by Andrew Clemson

'A Practical Guide to the Law of Gender Pay Gap Reporting' by Harini Iyengar

'NHS Whistleblowing and the Law' by Joseph England

'Employment Law and the Gig Economy' by Nigel Mackay & Annie Powell

'A Practical Guide to Noise Induced Hearing Loss (NIHL) Claims' by Andrew Mckie, Ian Skeate, Gareth McAloon

'An Introduction to Beauty Negligence Claims – A Practical Guide for the Personal Injury Practitioner' by Greg Almond

'Intercompany Agreements for Transfer Pricing Compliance' by Paul Sutton

'Zen and the Art of Mediation' by Martin Plowman

'A Practical Guide to Adoption for Family Lawyers' by Graham Pegg

'A Practical Guide to Industrial Disease Claims' by Andrew Mckie & Ian Skeate
'A Practical Guide to Conducting a Sheriff Court Proof' by Andrew Stevenson
'A Practical Guide to Vicarious Liability' by Mariel Irvine
'A Practical Guide to Applications for Landlord's Consent and Variation of Leases' by Mark Shelton
'A Practical Guide to Relief from Sanctions Post-Mitchell and Denton' by Peter Causton
'A Practical Guide to Equity Release for Advisors' by Paul Sams
'A Practical Guide to Financial Services Claims' by Chris Hegarty
'A Practical Guide to Financial Ombudsman Service Claims' by Adam Temple & Robert Scrivenor
'A Practical Guide to Running Housing Disrepair and Cavity Wall Claims – Second Edition' by Andrew Mckie & Ian Skeate
'A Practical Guide to Holiday Sickness Claims – Second Edition' by Andrew Mckie & Ian Skeate
'Arguments and Tactics for Personal Injury and Clinical Negligence Claims' by Dorian Williams
'A Practical Guide to Drone Law' by Rufus Ballaster, Andrew Firman, Eleanor Clot
'On Experts: CPR35 for Lawyers and Experts' by David Boyle
'An Introduction to Personal Injury Law' by David Boyle

These books and more are available to order online direct from the publisher at www.lawbriefpublishing.com, where you can also read free sample chapters. For any queries, call us on 0844 587 2383 or email us at mail@lawbriefpublishing.com.

Our books are all generally in stock at www.amazon.co.uk with free next day delivery for Prime members, and at good legal bookshops such as Wildy & Sons.

We are regularly launching new books in our series of practical day-to-day practitioners' guides. Visit our website and join our free newsletter to be kept informed and to receive special offers, free chapters, etc.

You can also follow us on Twitter at www.twitter.com/lawbriefpub.

www.ingramcontent.com/pod-product-compliance
Lightning Source LLC
LaVergne TN
LVHW022054200926
848481LV00003B/905